Emerging Risk in
International Banking

Emerging Risk in International Banking

ORIGINS OF FINANCIAL VULNERABILITY IN THE 1980s

P. N. Snowden

Department of Economics, University of Lancaster

London
GEORGE ALLEN & UNWIN
Boston   Sydney

George Allen & Unwin (Publishers) Ltd,
40 Museum Street, London WC1A 1LU, UK

George Allen & Unwin (Publishers) Ltd,
Park Lane, Hemel Hempstead, Herts HP2 4TE, UK

Allen & Unwin, Inc.,
Fifty Cross Street, Winchester, Mass. 01890, USA

George Allen & Unwin Australia Pty Ltd,
8 Napier Street, North Sydney, NSW 2060, Australia

First published in 1985.

Library of Congress Cataloging in Publication Data

Snowden, P. N. (P. Nicholas)
  Emerging risk in international banking.
1. Banks and banking, International.   2. Capital movements.
I. Title.
HG3891.S66   1985   332.1'5   85-7444
ISBN 0-04-332098-8 (alk. paper)

British Library Cataloguing in Publication Data

Snowden, P. N.
  Emerging risk in international banking: origins of financial
vulnerability in the 1980s.
1. Banks and banking, International   2. Risk
I. Title
332.1'5   HG3881
ISBN 0-04-332098-8

Set in 10 on 11 point Times by Fotographics (Bedford) Ltd,
and printed in Great Britain by Biddles Ltd, Guildford, Surrey

To the memory of my father
Frederick C. Snowden,
for showing me the firm ground,
and to that of Charles.

Contents

Acknowledgements

I wish to express appreciation to colleagues at Lancaster who shouldered the extra teaching and other duties during my period of sabbatical leave in 1981. Most of all I thank Baloo (V. N. Balasubramanyam) for his initiatives and encouragement without which a difficult period of gestation would have been much the more so.

A fundamental source of help was the research grant provided by the Economic and Social Research Council (B00230017/1). This enabled the author to have discussions with academics and staff of the IBRD and the International Monetary Fund (IMF) in the United States during early 1981. At the formative stage, these were the vital ingredients.

I recall with much appreciation my conversations with Jonathan Eaton, Mark Gersovitz and Peter Kenen at Princeton. Helpful also were Nick Hope at the IBRD and Jacques Artus at the IMF. Most especially Chandra Hardy of the International Bank for Reconstruction and Development was responsible for focusing the attention of the author on the need to investigate the behaviour of individual banks in seeking an understanding of the limits of sovereign lending. Although she (and all others named) is entirely blameless for the contents, without my discussion with her the project would not have evolved as it did.

My thanks are also due to both Jane Peill and Vanessa Graveson for typing the manuscript. The relief at seeing the transformation they were able to effect was considerable.

Finally, although aware that it is usually regarded as a formality, I note that without the happiness and encouragement I have derived from my wife Anne, and my daughters Frances and (very recently) Alexandra, the effort involved in the project would have been difficult to sustain.

Introduction
Risk and instability in international bank lending: aims of the study

On 20 August 1982, Mexico suspended payment for ninety days on its external debts of around $80 billion.[1] For a period thereafter, international financial markets were frozen to many less developed country borrowers (LDCs). Brazil, in particular, was precipitated into debt rescheduling on a similar scale to that which was hurriedly arranged for Mexico. The short term impact on these countries has been severe, with contractionary adjustment policies the *quid pro quo* of the rescheduling arrangements. In this way the early 1980s witnessed a culmination of the process which, as recycling, in the 1970s had supplied loans and permitted continued growth for certain LDCs, despite the oil price ramifications acting on the world economy.

Concern with the debt crisis has been on two levels. First, considerable attention has been paid, by international institutions as well as others, to the prospects facing major debtors (e.g. International Monetary Fund, 1984; Cline, 1984). What room do they have for resumed growth, for instance, given their repayment obligations? The second level has been concern over the safety of the international banking system given the possibility that one, or a few, major country borrowers could have approached the position of outright default. In this context the focus of concern has been the relative magnitude of some of these country loans, relative to the capital of the banks which have made them.

This volume is aimed at the second issue. The intention is to provide, as systematically as possible, an explanation of the processes by which the banks have accumulated such risks. Why have banks permitted country loans to become such a large fraction of their capital that bank insolvency appears as a serious possibility?

The answers generally provided to this question all appear potentially important, but have been presented in an *ad hoc* manner and do not provide a particularly satisfying overview of the process. Our motivation for attempting the exercise, other than clarification itself, has been to understand the sources of instability in bank intermediation in this context. In the view of the present writer the arguments suggest that present day temporary involvement in country lending by the International Monetary Fund (IMF) and the IBRD should increasingly become permanent.

The bulk of the explanation offered is contained in Chapters 4, 5 and 6, with the first three chapters providing contextual material. The emphasis in these early pages is on the relationship between 'real' international developments and the financial patterns which accompanied them. The basic enquiry is concerned with what fuelled the demand for international finance and how it was supplied. The answer to this is useful in showing the relative position of bank finance but also serves to emphasize that crises of finance are fundamentally interrelated with crises in real economic activity.

That economic crises and debt crises are usually related is well known historically both within national economies and in the field of international borrowing. As Kindleberger has argued from a review of historical experience:

> Maintaining debt service during world recession is generally impossible. Where countries have made serious efforts to do so – in Germany until the standstill agreement of July 1931 and in the Soviet Union with its relatively small debts through the 1930s – the results have been thoroughly unsatisfactory: the rise in totalitarianism out of mass unemployment on the one hand, and mass starvation through diversion of grain from cities to exports on the other. [Kindleberger, 1978, p. 9.]

Similarly, in more recent international economic relations there has been argued to be a correlation between the pattern of economic activity and the level of financial risk. Wallich (1978), for instance, suggested that (in the context of policy proposals for co-ordinated global economic reflation) there is a 'trade-off' between the minimization of financial risk and the maximization of returns to investment. The most recent example of his point has been the ability of the USA to borrow heavily on world capital markets. The financial risks to bankers and others (neglecting exchange risks) of lending to the US government are presumably small. It is a paradox, however, that a capital-rich country should be importing large volumes of financial capital from poorer nations where capital is fundamentally more scarce. Arguments for the efficiency of resource allocation would suggest a flow which is the opposite of those which appear to be the result of considerations of financial risk and return.

From an analytical viewpoint, however, the relationship between economic and financial (debt) crises has only incompletely been worked out. Perhaps the most suggestive analysis has been propounded by Minsky, basing a theory of national debt–deflation cycles on the earlier writings of Fisher. Although Minsky is thinking of national economic cycles, some elements of his analysis may be helpful in the present context.

His cycle begins with a 'general recognition' that a state of 'overindebtedness' exists from the point of view of debtors, or creditors, or both. The subsequent attempt to liquidate this debt leads to a diminution both of financial intermediation and of real activity. The depression factors lead to bankruptcies, a fall in nominal interest rates, and a rise in real ones. In explaining the emergence of an initial state of overindebtedness, Minsky argues that in the boom (upswing) *systematic shifts in the financial structure of business firms take place.* Rising optimism tempts firms to adopt a riskier financial structure by expanding debt in relation to owners' equity capital. The rising debt, and frequently shortening maturity, requires a steady, large cash flow for financing purposes. A diminution of the cash flow can therefore push many firms to the point of bankruptcy and such events trigger the debt–deflation cycle.

Although overindebtedness must be seen, fundamentally, as a relative concept, linked to the wealth or income flows accruing to the borrower, difficulties can arise even if the debt is not excessive *ex ante* on these criteria. Thus, Minsky argues, it is not only the magnitude of the debt but the time profile of repayment streams. Short term debt, for instance, presents more difficulty than long term debt since repayment streams involve interest and principal sums due. This outflow must be compared with the cash flow arising from the activities they have financed. Thus, in the situation where enterprises have incurred short term debt, in the process of financing long term investments, difficulties can rapidly multiply. For instance, a rise in interest rates both *increases* the short term cash outflow and *reduces* the present value of future income streams.

> For any given cash receipts due to assets and income production and payment commitments due to the liability structure there is an outer limit to interest rates that will preserve adequate margins of safety for the normal functioning of borrowing and lending. [Minsky, 1982, p. 383.]

This critical interest rate declines as the ratio of debt to equity in the financial structure is increased. Increasingly fairly small changes in interest rates, or opposite movements in profits, can produce the crisis turning point. Finally, innovations in finance are at the centre of Minsky's modern reformulation of the Fisher process. In the domestic context, financial innovation, by widening funding alternatives, tends to increase the price of capital assets and to reduce interest rates. The margin of safety referred to above widens, so encouraging more speculative financial structures.

The relevance of all this to the recent evolution of sovereign lending may be judged from the following quotation. After noting that international borrowing in the 1970s had been associated with a higher level of investment spending, the IMF staff express anxiety that difficulties could emerge if these investment projects turn out to be insufficiently productive in view of debt service obligations:

> . . . an unexpected shift in underlying external conditions rendered previously viable investment less profitable. For instance, the low or negative real rates of interest that prevailed during 1974–78, together with the expectations that such rates would continue, probably encouraged a higher level of external borrowing than would have occurred if the significantly positive real rates of interest that emerged from 1979 onward had been expected. [IMF, 1984, p. 63.]

In seeking an understanding of the basis of the current fears over world banking risk, the Minsky analysis alerts us, in particular, to two features of an emerging financial crisis. First there is the pattern of accumulation of financial liabilities by borrowers, especially the growth of debt relative to other sources of finance. It is such patterns which lie behind the sensitivity of the borrower to changed external circumstances, in our particular context, to the change in global real interest rates towards substantial positive real values after a period of their being negative. This important development is tied up with the change towards financial restriction in the major economies together with the lag in adjustment of inflation expectations in those countries in recent years.

Secondly, and this is the major point of departure of the present analysis, the nature of innovation in financial markets is held, by Minsky, to be of substantial importance. While changing interest rate structures, and other strains acting on the balance of payments, may help to trigger financing difficulties for particular country borrowers, an analysis of the development of the intermediation process is required to explain rising risk within the banking system.

Given these clues, the plan of the volume is as follows. In the first chapter the context of global economic developments in the 1970s is reviewed with attention given to current account patterns and attendant financing implied. The focus of the review is the disparate experience of differing country groups following the oil price shocks. The second chapter asks how far the patterns of financial flows to major borrowers changed over the period, with particular attention paid to the relative position of the banks. This allows an assessment of the relevance, or otherwise, of the first part of the Minsky theory as sketched above: that financial crises are associated with changing patterns of finance carrying with them increasing risk.

As Minsky's and Fisher's analyses stress, the borrowing must be seen relative to potential inflows to the borrower and an important part of the second chapter is the assessment of an explanation recently provided for the pattern of current account imbalances, and hence of financing needs, in the 1970s. This thesis stresses 'investment shifts' with the emergence of certain LDCs as borrowers reflecting their enhanced attractiveness as locations for investment spending relative to the major economies. Such an argument would offer a sanguine view of growing indebtedness since earnings streams would also be expected to grow. The conclusion of the chapter is that some evidence for investment shifts does exist but that country experience has been too variable, particularly on the savings side. This is taken to imply that domestic policies must also have had an important role to play. Before this argument is confronted with the two case studies of Chapter 3 a further more general point is made in Chapter 2. This is that assessing the strains imposed by high and rising interest rates requires allowance for the national patterns of indebtedness as well as for the impact on the real value of debt of world inflation throughout the period of the study. Much of the conclusion of this part of the analysis is indeed fairly sanguine about the existence of true overindebtedness generally. Where the Minsky thesis might find support, however, is in the countries which, in the 1970s, were the chief beneficiaries of international financial innovation in banking. In contrast to some surprisingly successful adjustments in East and South East Asia, Chapter 2 traces the emergence of Latin America as the main focus of the debt crisis. This in turn gives added weight to the choice of Brazil and Chile as the case studies of Chapter 3. As is clear the impact of external events has been particularly severe for these debtors, but deficiencies of domestic policies as much as growing investment, in one of the cases, must be seen as partly responsible for the rapid build up of international indebtedness.

Given varying ingredients in explaining the growing debt of different countries, Chapter 4 begins the main part of the analysis by taking up the second theme of the Fisher–Minsky argument. Here the nature of the contemporaneous financial developments of the 1970s are analysed. The prodigious growth of international credit is explained together with the importance of the major disparity which emerged, and stimulated bank intermediation. The disparity in question is between the liquidity preference of many of the newly rich oil-producing states and the desire for debt *illiquidity* by the emerging borrowers.

Since maturity transformation is a traditional function of banking it is not surprising that banks stepped in to meet the requirements of lenders and borrowers. It is noted, however, that the mechanics of this maturity transformation differ from those of domestic retail banking and have enhanced, thereby, the importance of linkages *between banks*. The role of the inter-bank market and potential system-wide risks are considered at this point.

These, however, are second order risks since maturity transformation will only present a problem in the face of a crisis of confidence rendering some intermediaries' ability to refinance their loan portfolios open to doubt. Since the difficulties of individual institutions could have system-wide ramifications, not only through inter-bank dealings, the focus switches in Chapters 5 and 6 to the apparently enhanced risks of banks. Chapter 5 considers the forces which persuaded banks to exploit their comparative advantage in maturity transformation and make such large commitments to sovereign lending. The context here is an analysis of loan markets where lenders' assessments of default probabilities are a crucial part of the equilibrium achieved. What made banks so sanguine in this regard? Chapter 6, which is to be seen as complementary with Chapter 5, seeks, none the less, to take the analysis further. What forces were acting on *individual banks* and what did they do? How far did they adjust to rising perceived risk? In particular, what was the role of banking competition in the choices made by these banks? It is contended that a key ingredient in the reduced perception of risk in sovereign lending, so important in the narrative of Chapter 5, was in fact due to the sequential nature of the banking competition that took place in this apparently lucrative business. It is further argued that the role of banking regulation in the United States could have been significant in this context as well as helping to precipitate overseas lending in the first place.

The final chapter addresses itself, in a deliberately unambitious way, to the need to maintain the availability of bank funding to the borrowing requirements of LDCs. The criterion used is that the developments envisaged should be immediately feasible given the actual circumstances of the present decade.

NOTES

1   All references to dollars imply the US dollar unless otherwise specified.
2   At the extreme a country would repudiate its debt ceasing to acknowledge service obligations. More or less serious default arises when the original terms cannot be adhered to despite the borrower's continuing recognition of these obligations.

1 Changing current account patterns in the 1970s

From the point of view of efficiency of resource allocation a flow of capital from capital-rich to capital-poor nations could be expected as a normal state of affairs. Such inflows on capital account would provide finance for current account deficits, the latter reflecting a rate of investment spending in excess of domestic saving. Countries would be expected to borrow on the basis of this investment motive provided that rates of interest on world capital markets remained below the marginal returns to new investment projects within the countries concerned.

In attempting to interpret the pattern of current account balances between countries in the 1970s it is useful to note that such surpluses or deficits reflect financing decisions on the capital account. While the actual pattern of financial flows in the decade is the subject of the next chapter, a brief review of motives behind international borrowing will be presented here. Other than the investment motive for international borrowing at least two other motives can be identified. These have been called the 'consumption' and the 'adjustment' motives (Eaton and Gersovitz, 1980). Having defined them, the chapter will go on to employ the terms in a consideration of the special requirements thrown up by the oil price increases of 1973–4 and 1978–80.

It will be seen that the 'adjustment motive' in this new context shades into the motive for investment and further emphasis will be given to investment for this reason. Additionally it has recently been suggested in the literature that the pattern of adjustment by the world economy to higher oil prices in fact reflects the enhanced importance of the investment motive behind the flow of funds to LDCs. This new view, which may be of fundamental importance, will be outlined in this chapter and assessed critically in the next. It is an argument which goes beyond the immediate impact of the oil crisis.

How then may a country justify borrowing for purposes of consumption? In the first instance, a country anticipating rapid income growth in future years may wish to borrow and allow consumption to rise in the present period against the 'security' of the growing income stream. Perhaps more usually, a country facing relatively sharp swings of its year on year income around a stable trend may want to borrow to smooth its consumption patterns between years. Such may be the situation of a primary exporting country dependent on world market conditions facing a small number of commodities, and it is for such purposes that the compensatory financing facility evolved within the IMF.

In contrast to the cases of the investment motive and the first consumption motive, where indebtedness tends to rise rapidly in the early years, the consumption 'smoothing' motive would not be expected to change the country's overall indebtedness over the course of a full cycle. In reality, of course, the two consumption motives do share a complication of which the investment motive is theoretically free. Whereas a viable investment financed by foreign funds generates its own income from which service payments (interest and amortization) can be extracted, the repayments associated with consumption loans of either type must be met from the government's general budget. In principle the service payments would be a prior charge on government revenue and if international indebtedness is rising as a fraction of national income, as for instance in the early years of the first consumption motive mentioned, tax revenues will gradually have to rise as a fraction of income, or other public spending will have to be cut, in order to meet the service payments involved (Newlyn, 1977, p. 102).

A similar prior charge on government revenues is generated by the borrowing undertaken for the adjustment motive. The need for adjustment might arise due to a cumulative loss of international competitiveness leading to a balance of payments crisis. Immediate application of measures to deal with the situation would probably involve severe domestic deflation together with exchange rate depreciation. The use of international borrowing, in such instances typically from the IMF credit tranches, would enable the country to undertake the necessary adjustments over a somewhat longer period, thus avoiding the worse 'stagflationary' effects. It is to be hoped that relatively small adjustments to the country's resource allocation in favour of the foreign trade sector would suffice.

What then were the salient features of the adjustment motive for international borrowing in the aftermath of the oil price increase? Unlike the more traditional need for balance of payments support, often provided and supervised by the IMF during adjustment of domestic economic policies, the requirement was for adjustment to an *exogenous* change in countries' international trading positions. That is, there was an impairment of import capacity over the medium term reflecting a fall in real national income. Secondly, again in contrast to the earlier adjustment problem, the need, although varying with differing national circumstances, was imposed *simultaneously* on a large number of countries. Thirdly, both exogenously and simultaneously, the export prospects facing LDCs markedly deteriorated as world economic growth declined in the years subsequent to the formation of OPEC (the Organization of Petroleum Exporting Countries).

In the aftermath of the first oil price increases between 1973 and 1978 the oil-exporting countries used about half of their increased real resources in the purchase of goods and services primarily from developed countries (DCs). The other major development, quantitatively, however, was that the industrial countries reduced their rates of economic growth. On the average they were some 2.5 percentage points below the Organization for Economic Co-operation and Development (OECD) growth rates of the preceding decade (IMF, 1980, p. 74). By no means all of this reduction was the direct result of the rise in oil prices and, indeed, counter-inflation policies and issues relating to declining productivity growth in the developed countries were probably crucial. None the less, the oil price increases rendered difficult policy issues the more intractable. The outcome was that a collective deficit on the OECD countries' balance of payments of some $8 billion in 1973 had been converted into a surplus of some $30 billion by 1978. As the World Bank (IBRD) comments,

> . . . reduced deficits are not themselves evidence of successful adjustment; if they are achieved simply by slowing down activity, they underwrite the contractionary effect of higher oil prices. [IBRD, 1981, p. 9.][1]

For a number of reasons, some of which, like declining productivity trends, may be fundamentally long lasting, the developed world responded in a quite conventional way to the deterioration of its trade balances experienced during the 1970s. In discussing the appropriateness or otherwise of this response, given our focus, it is not intended to discuss directly the efficiency of the counter-inflation strategy that has come to dominate policy making in many of the major industrial nations. From the point of view of the global economy, however, one point should be emphasized. The rise in real income of the oil-producing nations was matched by a decline in the current real income of the oil-importing nations. It was therefore appropriate that the domestic absorption of goods and services by these latter countries should be curtailed, but this does not mean that a general deflationary policy was appropriate on these grounds. The key to this point lies in the fact that *world* real income had not been reduced but rather redistributed in favour of oil producers who were inclined to accumulate financial assets with a substantial fraction of their increased income. Deflation of the world economy was therefore not called for; instead global adjustment needed to be in the form of a shift from consumption spending towards investment spending to match the increased potential supply of loanable funds.

If, for a moment, however, we visualize the world economy as two blocks, the global deflation that actually occurred can be seen in terms of the more traditional theoretical concern with the 'transfer problem'. This was initially concerned with the conditions under which attempts by one nation to transfer real resources to another, by making financial provision to do so, would in fact be successful after economic ramifications had been taken into account. After World War I German reparation payments to the victorious countries were a crucial early area of application of this theory.

In the present context the possibility of 'global' deflation, given sufficiently high incremental savings ratios out of transfer receipts in relation to the propensity to spend these receipts on imports, is established at least in a Keynesian framework (Johnson, 1958). As the oil-exporting countries had high marginal propensities to save out of their extra 'transfer' income and as their import spending, at least initially, was low, the deflationary results would be understandable. As Johnson's analysis indicates, the role of capital movements between the two groups becomes important in determining the final outcome.

On this interpretation of events it would have been quite feasible for world output growth to continue undiminished following the rise in oil prices. While the rise in energy costs may have reduced the increment to output for each unit of investment spending (as more expensive plant was ordered to economize on fuel), the rise in availability of investment funds should have at least compensated for this effect. Against this background, what in fact happened to the growth performance of the world economy?

The slowing of growth is most clearly marked in the main industrial countries. Whereas, during the 1960s, they had grown at around 5 per cent a year, the rate dropped to an average of 3.3 per cent during the 1970s.

Table 1.1 shows the analytical subgroupings used by the IMF in its global report. 'Net oil exporters' are countries whose oil exports (net of any imports of crude oil) did not amount to two-thirds of their total exports and did not amount to 100 million barrels a year (IMF, 1980, p. 24). This would include countries like Mexico, Egypt, Gabon and Bolivia. The low income countries are thirty-eight in number with 1977 per capita gross domestic product (GDP) below $300, India

Table 1.1   *Percentage changes in output 1973–81*

	1973	1974	1975	1976	1977	1978	1979	1980	1981	Previous averages[a]
Industrial (OECD) countries (GNP)	6.3	0.7	–0.6	5.2	3.9	4.0	3.7	1.2	1.5	4.8
Non-oil developing countries (GDP)										
(1) Net oil exporters	7.5	6.1	5.3	4.8	3.2	5.8	7.1	6.7	6.8	6.0
(2) Net oil importers	6.0	5.5	3.7	5.5	5.1	5.5	4.5	4.0	4.6	5.8
(2a) Major exporters of manufactures	9.5	6.6	3.3	6.1	5.1	5.2	6.5	4.7	4.6	8.1
(2b) Low income countries	2.9	3.2	5.7	3.4	4.7	6.0	0.2	3.1	4.9	3.4
(2c) Other net oil importers	4.1	6.0	2.6	6.4	5.4	5.6	4.1	3.4	4.1	5.5

Source: IMF (1981), Tables 1 and 2, pp. 111–2.
[a] Industrial countries = 1962–72; non oil-developing countries = 1967–72.

excluded. India is added to the 'major exporters of manufactures' group. This includes most of the middle income countries and newly industrialized countries (NICs). There are twelve such manufacturing exporters including India and interestingly they account for well over three-fifths of the combined GDP or total exports of all oil-importing LDCs. This compares with only 12 per cent and 6.7 per cent respectively for the thirty-eight low income countries. The remainder are fifty middle income countries (GDP per capita in excess of $300 in 1977) whose exports are mainly of primary commodities.

As may have been expected, the data suggests that the net oil exporters managed to maintain a rather strong growth performance. Compared with previous averages the net oil importers displayed a marked slackening following 1976 from around 6 per cent to 5 per cent. Of the subgroups it seems probable that the low income countries fared least well with some of the larger Asian states masking, in the averages shown, a rather severe deterioration in the smallest countries. If the 1960s are compared with the 1970s per capita income growth rates for this group declined from 1.8 per cent to 0.8 per cent.

The middle income countries comprising groups 2a and 2c in Table 1.1 performed well in comparison with both the industrial countries and the low income group. Thus gross national product (GNP) per person in the two groups averaged a 3.1 per cent growth in the 1970s in contrast with 3.6 per cent in the 1960s

From a global point of view, then, a significant part of the adjustment to higher oil prices occurred in the form of reduced rates of growth, most notably in the OECD nations and, most painfully, in some of the lowest income countries. However, it is noteworthy that the middle income LDCs, and particularly the major exporters of manufactures, sustained fairly strong although somewhat diminished growth performances even in the wake of the second round of oil price increases. A major question to be addressed in the next two chapters therefore will be whether or not the adjustment in these countries followed the ostensibly desirable path of a shift toward a higher rate of investment spending together with a curtailment of consumption. What is important for the present, however, is that the middle income countries were sustaining a *relatively* impressive growth performance in these difficult years. Pending closer investigation, the earlier discussion suggests that this was 'justifiable' growth in the sense of adjustment to higher oil prices. Chapter 3 will examine this 'dynamic' adjustment process for two countries.

What do such modes of adjustment imply for international indebtedness? If countries are going to draw on the oil-based source of savings, the implication, of course, is that current account payment deficits would be the norm and must be financed by borrowing. Provided that the deficits were being generated by a sufficiently large increment to investment spending, the borrowing would represent sound adjustment by the countries concerned. These investments would provide the basis for the ultimate repayment of interest and principal when the oil-exporting nations gradually began to spend their accumulated reserves. From this point of view the physical location of the investments concerned would be of little consequence.

It is certainly the case that the distribution of the deficits between DCs and LDCs was extremely skewed. As a group the oil importing LDCs had a $7 billion current account deficit in 1973 which leapt to $33 billion in 1974 and $39 billion in 1975 (representing 5.2 per cent of total GDP). This trend was ameliorated in 1978 when the deficit fell to $26 billion following some recovery in the OECD nations. As we have seen, the OECD nations responded to the oil price rises directly or indirectly by curtailing economic activity and moving back, as a group, surprisingly quickly to current account surplus. The underlying reasons for this were that an apparent increase in 'inflation-proneness' within those nations led to a commitment by the authorities there to use fiscal and monetary policy to reduce inflation as a prime strategy. This in turn curtailed both consumption and investment spending.

The result was that the payments deficits implied by the OPEC surpluses percolated down to the LDCs as a group. Moreover, the potential deficit facing these countries was even larger, reflecting, in addition to the rise in oil prices which we have discussed, a significant reduction in demand for their exports in the major OECD nations. The reverse of this effect is part of the explanation for the improved LDC payment balance quoted above for 1978. That there was a slow-down in the rate of growth of the developing countries is unsurprising given this extra complication. A more precise indication of the impact of this extra external shock to which some adjustment had to be made has again been provided by the World Bank. The World Bank decomposes developments in the net barter terms of trade[2] into export and import price effects. These are then related through export and import volumes into percentages of GNP. In addition, the shock attributable to a slowing in the growth of OECD export markets is calculated as the difference between *projected* volumes into 1974–8 on the basis of growth rates over the period 1963–73, and the actual volumes realized in the years 1974–8. The 1974–8 averages of the price and volume effects are given separately in Table 1.2.

The negative signs are to be taken as the *beneficial* effect of export price rises exceeding the growth of world trade prices of manufactured products. They therefore represent the increased purchasing power of a given quantity of exports over such items. The import price rises, on the other hand, reflect the excess over the same datum with oil prices being the crucial factor.

The differing groups represent a similar classification to that used by the IMF as noted above except that India, Pakistan and Bangladesh are given the separate subgroup of 'Populous South Asia'.

The relative strength of the price and volume effects is similar for the semi-industrial and primary producing groups. For the subcontinent countries price effects dominated whereas the reverse was significantly the case for the low income group. Interestingly the relative immunity of the subcontinent to volume shortfalls was substantially attributable to the success of India and Pakistan in selling a large part of their merchandise exports directly to other developing countries rather than to the depressed OECD [IBRD, 1981 p. 66].

It appears from these figures that the volume effects reflecting the slowing of world trade had a strong impact on most of the developing

Table 1.2   *Trade price and export volume 'shocks' to groups of oil importing developing countries: average percentages of GNP 1974–8*

		Semi-industrial	Primary producing	Populous South Asia	Least developed
(1)	International price effects	0.9	1.65	1.26	0.14
(1a)	Export price effects	–0.83	–3.21	–0.19	–2.07
(1b)	Import price effects	1.73	4.86	1.45	2.21
(2)	Export volume effects	0.91	1.99	0.69	1.39
Total 1+2		1.81	3.64	1.95	1.53

Source: IBRD (1981), Table 6.2, p. 66.

country subgroups. The curtailment of economic activity in the OECD nations tended directly to worsen the trade prospects of the poor nations already facing a terms of trade deterioration.

Not only did the trade deficits concentrate in the developing world, however, but within the LDCs the distribution of the deficits was very uneven. Thus:

> Approximately two-thirds of both the developing countries' debt and debt service obligations are accounted for by thirteen major borrowers. Of these, six are important exporters of manufactures (Argentina, Brazil, Israel, Korea, Spain and Yugoslavia) and five are exporters of petroleum (Algeria, Egypt, Indonesia, Mexico and Venezuela). The other two are India and Turkey; India is the only one of the thirteen that is a low income country and almost all of its debt is from official sources, mostly on concessional terms. [IBRD, 1981, p. xvii.]

These comments will be amplified in the next chapter where the financing of deficits on current account will be considered together with the specific position of a number of countries mentioned in this quotation. However from the preceding discussion it is not apparent why net exporters of petroleum should be found amongst the major borrower LDCs. We have so far been talking in the most general terms of the oil-producers' surpluses automatically being reflected in deficits for developed and less developed oil importers. Evidently, however, when we begin to consider the actual *distribution* of the deficits within these groups there seems to be no close correspondence between countries' dependence on imported oil and the magnitude of their total borrowing. This turns out to be true also for the developed countries (Sachs, 1981). What, therefore, do the distribution of deficits and the attendant international borrowing patterns represent? The view consistent with what has been said so far is that the developed countries generally responded by restrictive economic policies aimed at reducing inflationary impulses of various kinds, only some of which were directly related to the oil price increases. Deficits corresponding to OPEC surpluses were therefore concentrated in the non-oil LDCs that had retained a commitment to economic growth. The distribution of the deficits within these groups could be explained by the relative strengths of contractionary policies followed by the various OECD nations, together with these countries' successes in penetrating new export markets. Thus, Japan and West Germany retained a stronger external position than the United States. Similarly, the more credit-worthy middle income LDCs were able to 'spread' the shock of the oil price rises by borrowing against the 'security' of their growth potential. On this view the distribution of deficits among the LDCs would be substantially explained by their capacity for 'adjustment' in the context of growth. The maintenance of a sufficiently high rate of investment spending relative to consumption would be crucial in this respect.

The last part of this argument suggests that *internal* policy responses by certain LDCs were a part of the explanation, as well as the initiating terms of trade and export volume effects we have already discussed. This does, in fact, appear to have been the case. A recent study has attempted to 'explain' the pattern of LDC current account deficits on international payments by reference to a number of external and internal influences. As emerging payments deficits have occasioned the international indebtedness we are discussing, the results of the study are of direct interest. Kahn and Knight (1983) utilize data from a sample of thirty-two non-oil LDCs over the years 1973–81. In line with our earlier discussion they relate the deficit to terms of trade effects as well as to export volume impacts; the latter represented by an index of growth in the OECD nations. It should be noted, here, that terms of trade are affected by more than just oil prices and, as Table 1.2 indicated, LDCs were able to recoup somewhat from a general improvement in the relative prices of primary commodities, especially, as it happens, in the years of the oil price increases. In general, these prices are heavily influenced by the economic conditions in the OECD countries. In other words, weakness in the economies of these major markets has an additional depressing effect on the terms of trade of LDCs and, to this extent, the terms of trade and OECD activity measures are related. Another major influence working on primary commodity prices, however, was the general adjustment to high global inflation so that when this, and the oil price changes, are recognized, the correspondence between the two measures is not close.

A further 'external' influence in Kahn and Knight's regression is the level of real interest rates in international capital markets since these will affect interest payments on existing debt incorporated in the current account. As will be seen in the next chapter these varied considerably over the period, with varying implications for the current accounts of the debtor nations.

In addition to these external factors, the authors include two indicators of internal economic policy within the thirty-two countries. These are fiscal deficit as a percentage of nominal GDP, which represents the shortfall of government revenues from expenditure and the real effective exchange rate.

Kahn and Knight's reason for including the fiscal deficit rests on the correlation between excess domestic 'absorption' and a deficit on the current account. Since LDCs are characterized by inadequate domestic capital markets, government deficits tend either to be covered by borrowing from the domestic banking system, with inflationary consequences, or by borrowing on international capital markets. In either event the *current* account will tend to be driven into deficit. As the authors point out, the fiscal deficit : GDP ratio for non-oil LDCs was constantly positive in the period 1973–81, The ratio rose from approximately 2 per cent in 1973 to around 3.5 per cent in 1979–81. A slight improvement in the ratio in 1978 probably reflects the stronger economic performance in that year with its beneficial effects on government revenues.

While a fiscal deficit will lead to a deficit on current account if domestic sources of savings are inadequate, Kahn and Knight do not differentiate the type of government expenditure. Fiscal deficits, as well as representing absorption in excess of current resources, can also result directly, or indirectly, in an increase in capital formation. To the extent that this is the case and the investment is 'productive' the fiscal deficit may be less worrying. The next chapter will consider investment performance of LDCs in this period.

The final variable considered by Kahn and Knight is the real effective exchange rate. Arguing from evidence produced elsewhere, they suggest that inflation in LDCs tends to lead (through a failure of the exchange rate to reflect its relationship with world inflation) to an *appreciation* in the real effective rate. In consequence, exports tend to suffer a cost squeeze with negative consequences for supply and imports are cheapened for domestic users.

Results of the regression analysis suggest that all of the variables listed have played a part with the terms of trade coefficient explaining most of the variation. The foreign real interest rate, the real effective exchange rate and the government's fiscal position appear to be of equal consequence. An important corollary is that inappropriate *domestic* policies have had at least some influence on the distribution of LDC deficits. The regression equations suggest that an x per cent deterioration of the terms of trade could have been offset by a *successful* $0.9x$ per cent depreciation of the real effective exchange rate. The degree of success, of course, would depend on how far the authorities could prevent domestic costs rising to offset a depreciation of the *nominal* rate.

As these authors note, however, such a policy response would be most appropriate for *one* country on the assumption that most other LDCs did *not* follow its example! The larger the group that did so, the more likely it would be that the terms of trade of the group would deteriorate further as global supplies expanded in the face of low price elasticities of demand.

Although it seems to be the case that at least some countries were following overly expansionist domestic policies, which required adjustment of the type described, there remains the question of appropriate *global* adjustment. Borrowing, in so far as it could be justified by the ability to invest productively, would have to be a part of this answer.

In this connection, there has recently emerged a more dynamic view of the distribution of global payments deficits which sees the oil price increases as only one element in a picture where the distribution is dominated by shifts in global *investment* patterns. At the time of writing a part of this view seems suspect because it tends to assume that the rise in oil prices was seen as 'permanent' by the oil-consuming countries. That is, the fall in current incomes which we have discussed was assumed to persist into the future. On this 'permanent income' interpretation the rise in oil prices would not be expected to lead to payments deficits because the reduction in income would be matched by a reduction in absorption (notably consumption) as people adjusted to their lower anticipated real income streams. Moreover, investment spending would be reduced by the lower anticipated returns following the 'permanent' rise in the price of oil as an important input into the production process. As this lasting reduction in income streams would most seriously affect 'resource-poor' economies (like West Germany and Japan in contrast to the USA), these countries would be characterized by a strong position on their current account balances. This would be an alternative explanation of the patterns observed between the OECD nations.

While on the one hand a reduction in total OECD investment spending might have been anticipated. the OPEC nations could be expected to increase their savings (or accumulation of financial assets). The basic reason, in the spirit of the permanent income hypothesis, would be that even with a permanent rise in the oil price the depletion of reserves would induce the OPEC countries to seek to hold financial assets to smooth their projected consumption streams over the period when oil reserves began to decline. On the one hand then, there was a decline in investment spending in the OECD nations and, on the other, a rise in availability of global savings. World economic adjustment to this change would be completed, therefore, by a reduction in the average real level of interest rates. At the global level this equilibrating change in the level of rates would stimulate consumption and increase investment spending. There is indeed some evidence that real interest rates did fall after 1973 (Sachs, 1981, Table 8).

Whether or not this view of events is inherently superior to the rather more 'Keynesian' analysis presented earlier, it does focus on interpreting current account balances as the outcome of savings and investment decisions. Thus, whereas the anticipated returns to investment in the OECD nations arguably had been reduced by the oil price-associated developments, there is reason to believe that the prospects for investment spending in LDCs were becoming brighter. We will come to the reasons for this in a moment but, on the permanent income approach being discussed, an improvement in investment prospects would tend to lead to a current account deficit in the countries in which it was taking place. An enhanced growth potential would cause residents to spend more now in anticipation of higher rates of income growth in the future. Moreover the reduction in world interest rates would encourage countries to finance a part of their overall absorption (consumption plus investment spending) by borrowing on world capital markets.

According to this view, as in our previous analysis, LDCs with bright growth prospects could be expected to continue with substantial payments deficits and therefore to accumulate international indebtedness.

However, although OPEC-related changes are seen to be significant in explaining the pattern in which current account balances have been distributed, the focus is firmly on savings and investment decisions. According to one of the authors of this view, the weakening of OECD investment had three components. First, there was a weakening of the post World War II investment boom in many OECD economies (suggesting diminishing marginal returns to investment in the early 1970s). The technological gap between the USA and the rest of the OECD had been largely closed, while the increments to effective labour supply declined as the process of transferring labour from traditional sectors was completed.

Second, a sharp squeeze in profits appears to have affected most of the OECD economies in the 1970s. The result (of an acceleration of real wages) was a rise in labour's share of income and a fall in the pre-tax rate of return to corporate capital in many economies (Sachs, 1981, p. 238).

While Sachs also notes a third component, increased investment in raw material extraction of the type heavily concentrated in non-oil LDCs, he also points out that manufacturing investment had increased strongly in the more advanced non-oil LDCs. Whereas such factors have reduced the attractiveness of investment in developed countries, the middle income developing countries have frequently been altering their economic strategies in a direction which has raised the potential returns to capital in those countries. Most directly, financial liberalization and rationalization of import controls, tariffs and exchange rates have encouraged outward-looking trade policies based on comparative advantage. The conspicuous success of Korea, Taiwan and, to a more variable degree, Brazil can be mentioned here.

Irrespective of the merits of the permanent income view of the oil price increases, this argument concerning shifts in the relative attractiveness of investment in LDCs as opposed to the OECD economies is sufficiently interesting to merit further attention in Chapter 2. In terms of the argument presented above it suggests that the 'adjustment' motive for borrowing must now be seen as operating alongside the 'investment' motive. It is an argument which reinforces the basic proposition that developing countries need to be continuing net importers of capital irrespective of developments in world oil markets. Undoubtedly, however, the oil crisis has magnified payments imbalances and, accordingly, has increased the level of international borrowing that LDCs have been required to undertake. The impact on these countries of the 1973–4 oil price increases displayed in Table 1.2 was repeated with the 1978–80 increases. This more recent experience will be discussed in the next chapter.

NOTES

1   This source provides a number of the statistics quoted in the text.

2   Defined as

$$N = \frac{X p_t}{X p_0} \bigg/ \frac{M p_t}{M p_0}$$

where numerator and denominator are indices of export and import prices in year t with respect to a base year 0.

2 Global investment 'shifts' and financing patterns

The first chapter considered the influences leading to the increased borrowing by LDCs on world capital markets in the 1970s. Two features of the examination stand out. Firstly, the dominant influences on current account deficits, and (through the financing of a part of these) on the accumulation of international indebtedness, were oil price-induced real income losses *and* falls in export volume induced by recession in the OECD economies. As made clear in Table 1.2, the oil price effects would have been considerably more disruptive had not *favourable* price movements been recorded for other primary commodities. Taking this into account, export volume effects were equally as important in their impact on the LDCs as overall price influences.

The second important conclusion was that though the oil price increases had been important in determining the current account movements of *groups* of countries, the current accounts of individual countries had not been closely correlated with oil import dependence. In explaining the distribution of deficits between countries (LDCs) it was found that a number of additional influences had to be taken into account. As well as the extra external effect of real international interest rates on existing debt, which represent a current account outflow, domestic policy factors also appeared to be significant. In particular, government budget balances and exchange rate policies were significant in the statistical sense.

In the present chapter, these themes will be explored in rather more detail. The substantial current account shifts of the 1970s necessitated international financial flows of a differing order of magnitude from those of earlier years. Accordingly the external 'balance sheet' of countries' assets and liabilities has changed, in some cases substantially. Our concern now is to examine the *types* of funding used, to discern major relative changes and especially to place in context the growth of private bank involvement in international borrowing. A number of important themes emerge here with respect to the costs and benefits of differing types of finance. It will be seen that a critical factor in such an assessment concerns the impact of inflation on debt servicing.

On the second level we have identified, of the relevance of national policy to the accumulation of indebtedness, we give further consideration to the thesis that 'investment shifts' in favour of certain LDCs (the NICs) may explain a part of the increased levels of debt in those countries. It is in the context of these states that 'adjustment' to terms of trade losses might most reasonably take the form of enhanced investment spending financed by a temporary increase in debt. An important feature encouraging this strategy, it will be recalled, was argued to be the fall in real interest rates which accompanied the oil price increases and which will be enumerated in this chapter.

This 'dynamic adjustment' argument is important, since the countries for which it could most readily apply tend also to be the most heavily indebted to private banks. As such, any dangers of this type of finance must apply particularly to them. In turn the latter part of the present chapter will set the scene for the next when two of the countries concerned will have their economic performance more critically appraised.

The broad picture for the current account developments of recent years is given in Table 2.1. At this aggregate level, the correlated patterns of oil dependence and increase in current account deficit are apparent for 1974 and 1979–80. The increased magnitude of the current deficit in the industrial countries in 1980 reflects, in part, the deterioration of the position of West Germany, which in the earlier year was enjoying an export boom. Both West Germany and Japan, which experienced current account surpluses in much of the decade until 1979, initially financed the deficits in that year by running down reserve assets and thereby resisting currency depreciation. After this initial response these and other developed countries (DCs) sought to finance their continuing deficits by attracting private capital inflows. The decision to finance deficits in this way enhanced the requirement that interest rates be 'competitive' with those in the United States. This is one of the routes whereby monetary policy in the United States achieves a pervasive influence on the terms at which funds become available on international capital markets. That country's changed stance in 1979 ushered in a more general and sustained policy of monetary disinflation in the major economies. More substantial attempts were also made to cut oil consumption. The results listed in Table 1.1 for OECD growth rates in the early 1980s is evidence of widespread concern with inflation in the major economies. The small aggregate payments imbalances of 1981–3 in Table 2.1 are further evidence for this effect.

For the developing oil importers, the impact of the second round of

Table 2.1 *Payments balances on current account; country groupings 1973–84 ($ billions)*

	1973	1974	1975	1976	1977	1978	1979	1980	1981	1982	1983	1984
Industrial countries	19.3	-12.4	17.1	-2.1	-2.2	32.4	-5.4	-40.4	1.9	-1.4	-1.2	-22.5
Oil exporters	6.6	67.8	35.0	40.0	29.4	5.7	62.5	111.0	53.4	-12.0	-16.2	-8.0
Non-oil LDCs	-11.5	-36.8	-46.5	-32.9	-30.4	-42.7	-62.0	-87.7	-109.1	-82.2	-56.4	-50.0
of which Net oil exporters	-2.6	-5.1	-10.1	-7.8	-6.3	-7.4	-7.3	-10.2	-24.3	-14.4	-6.9	-9.5
Net oil importers	-8.9	-31.7	-36.5	-25.1	-25.0	-34.2	-52.5	-74.2	-86.1	-73.5	-54.5	-43.5

Source: IMF (1981), Statistical Appendix Table 14, p. 123 (years 1973–6 inclusive); IMF (1984), Statistical Appendix Table 17, p. 187 (years 1977 on).

The discrepancy arising between the Non-oil LDC totals and the two subgroups after 1977 is due to the exclusion of China (a net oil exporter) from the sub group.

Table 2.2 Non-oil LDCs: current account financing 1973–84 ($billions)

	1973	1974	1975	1976	1977	1978	1979	1980	1981	1982	1983	1984
(1) Current account deficit (cf. row 3, Table 2.1)	11.5	36.8	46.5	32.9	30.4	42.3	62.0	87.8	109.1	82.2	56.4	50.0
(2) Net non-debt-creating flows	10.4	12.8	12.0	11.9	14.1	17.0	23.7	24.1	27.2	23.9	21.3	23.0
of which (2a) Net direct investment	4.4	5.4	5.3	4.8	5.4	7.1	9.3	9.4	13.1	11.2	7.9	9.0
(3) Reserve accumulation (-ve)	-9.7	-2.3	1.8	-13.2	-11.5	-16.3	-11.8	-6.8	-5.4	3.8	-6.1	-13.3
(4) Recorded errors and omissions[a]	-5.3	-3.9	-3.9	-4.1	-6.5	-6.9	-3.0	-15.4	-15.5	-18.8	-10.0	-5.0
(5) Net external borrowing[b]	16.1	30.1	36.7	38.4	34.4	48.6	53.0	85.9	102.9	73.2	51.2	45.3
(6) Reserve-related liabilities[c]	—	1.5	2.3	3.7	2.9	2.0	-0.5	5.3	9.8	15.4	8.4	1.0
(7) Official long-term borrowing	5.7	9.9	11.7	10.8	13.1	13.8	17.0	20.0	22.6	21.6	22.6	23.1
(8) Other	10.4	18.6	22.7	23.9	18.4	32.8	36.5	60.6	70.5	36.2	20.2	21.2
of which (8a) from banks	9.0	12.3	13.2	16.1	6.8	22.0	23.3	27.8	28.8	15.7	40.2	35.6

Source: IMF (1981), Statistical Appendix Table 22, p. 129 (1973–6); IMF (1984), Statistical Appendix Table 28, p. 197 (1977–84).
[a] Following latest IMF practice residual flows and other errors have been excluded from net external borrowing for 1973–6 inclusive as they are assumed largely to represent capital *outflows*.
[b] Line 5 = line 1 – line 2 – (line 3) – (line 4) = the sum of lines 6, 7 and 8.
[c] Mainly the use of IMF credit and arrears on debt payments due.

oil price increases, along with the reduced activity in their major markets, is indicated by their enhanced current deficits. The financing of these deficits is given, on a comparable basis, in Table 2.2, again drawing on IMF sources. A complementary source is provided by the OECD in the form of an informative constant price series of financial flows to LDCs. These may be used in conjunction with Table 2.2 in the text and are presented as Tables A2.1 and A2.2 in the appendix to this chapter.

Returning to Table 2.2 the first clear change between 1973 and the end of the period is in the relative magnitude of net borrowing. In 1973 as in the years until then, the typical picture was of current account deficits financed by a combination of aid and direct investment. Aid comprises grants (non-repayable), which would be included in the second line of Table 2.2, and concessionary loans. These are not shown separately from non-concessionary official loans in line 7. According to the OECD data in Table A2.1, 72 per cent of official sources funds qualified as official development assistance (ODA), that is, grants or loans having a grant element of at least 25 per cent, in 1973. By 1982, the latest available year, the ratio was 60 per cent. The most significant growth of the remaining (non-concessionary) official financing was found in official and officially supported export credits and in non-concessionary finance from multilateral agencies. The latter would incorporate the World Bank with its market-related lending terms.

Another feature of the 1973 data is that long term lending from the private sector (notably from financial institutions, in rows 8 and 8a of Table 2.2) was already significant and sufficient to finance a substantial increase in the official reserves of LDCs. The OECD data demonstrate the importance of bank lending in the years 1970–3. In those figures capital market lending (being bank lending plus bond issues) amounted to $9 billion in 1970 and to $20 billion in 1973. Both these values are in constant prices and represent 17 per cent and 31 per cent of total resource receipts by the LDCs (OECD definition) respectively. Part of the reason for this was the commodity boom, but also developments in the international financial system, and particularly financial developments in the Eurocurrency markets (e.g. syndicated lending), all making banks more responsive to the demands of sovereign borrowers (OECD, 1983, p. 57). Such borrowing had allowed reserves to be built up.

What can be said about developments from 1973 through the oil crisis years shown in our tables? The gradual decline in the relative position of ODA, despite the fact that from all sources (including OPEC and the World Bank's International Development Association) ODA increased in real terms by 70 per cent between 1970 and 1982, has already been mentioned. As Table A2.2 shows, this relative decline was offset by a growth of official bilateral and multilateral non-concessional lending.

As can be seen from Table 2.2 and from those in the appendix to this chapter, direct private investment flows increased over the period, with the OECD data indicating that a real increase took place. Indeed, it appears that from 1975, flows of direct foreign private investment rather constantly exceeded the magnitudes typical of the earlier 1970s. This may be tentative support for the 'investment shifts' argument to be discussed below. Interestingly, however, as the OECD data shows (Table A2.2) the *relative* contribution from this source declined. The main reason was the rapid growth, in particular, of capital market lending. As the OECD report makes clear, between the beginning and end of the period in question the proportion of private (non-concessional) flows made up of direct investment and bank lending had been reversed. Whereas direct investment formed 20 per cent of resource transfers in 1970 and capital market finance represented 16 per cent, the ratios were 14 per cent and 23 per cent respectively in 1982.

Thus one of the most dramatic, and from our point of view interesting, developments in the period was the rapid relative growth of financing from private banks. One or two comments are called for, however, concerning the *way* in which bank lending grew, without at present considering its *distribution* between LDCs. The first point, made clear in the OECD data of Table A2.1 is that bank lending, which had been growing rapidly, tended to be reduced in the wake of the first oil crisis year of 1974. It appears that the earlier expansion of bank lending had permitted countries to build up substantial liquid reserves and the first impact of recycling was a running down, or decreased rate of accumulation of foreign exchange reserves. Table 2.2 above makes this clear. Thus, total bank intermediation did not rise whereas the ownership of existing deposits changed hands – e.g. from LDCs to OPEC governments. It appears that this was a rather general phenomenon (Stanyer and Whitley, 1981, pp. 191–2).

It was following 1975 that bank lending began to increase again in real terms (Table A2.1), a period which coincided with an improvement in LDC terms of trade Again, significantly from the point of view of the 'investment shifts' argument, OECD figures suggest that a new peak of real bank lending was reached in 1978 (i.e. prior to the second oil price increase). This also coincided with a relatively high level of foreign direct investment. Certainly, the years 1976–81 appear to have been characterized by a new high level of lending.

A tentative conclusion from this pattern would be that while bank lending was stimulated by the oil crisis, it was also stimulated by 'supply side' factors such as the earlier development of syndicated lending and the second phase of Eurocurrency market expansion witnessed in the later 1970s. Again as Table 2.2 shows, the build up of bank lending was associated with a renewed growth of foreign exchange reserves. Following 1979, the 1974 picture is repeated with a falling away of bank finance in 1980 and a substantially reduced rate of growth of foreign exchange reserves. It would be incorrect to suggest that bank lending was therefore not much affected by oil price increases, since the demand for reserves had something of a precautionary balance element contained in it. However, it does also appear to be true that bank lending to LDCs was available on highly attractive terms and, as such, induced those countries to hold increasing reserves. In view of evidence to be presented later about the behaviour of two of the major banks, much of the growth in bank lending after 1976 would indicate the rapid increase in 'new' banks expanding their overseas loans portfolios. One estimate was that an average 65 new 'names' per year were entering the syndicated loan markets at this time with the result that loan rate 'spreads' (over the cost of funds), declined from a 'high' in 1976 through to 1980 (Economist, 1982, pp. 77–8). This decline applied to both OECD and LDC loans.

For the post 1980 period the OECD figures suggest a significantly changed atmosphere with an apparent falling away of long term bank lending in 1982 and, in 1980–1 a substantial increase in short term bank borrowing. Moreover between 1980 and 1982 a marked recovery in loan rate 'spreads' took place with the *gap* between OECD and LDC loans widening markedly. The gap began to close again in 1982–3 as new loan volume declined, (Economist, 1984, p. 9). It is difficult to avoid the impression from recent years that the rapid expansion of bank involvement in LDC lending may have been a 'phase' (or perhaps two phases, up to 1973 and 1975–81), unlikely to be repeated with the same vigour as banks approach the limits of prudence in their portfolio composition. The market and institutional arrangements leading to this interpretation are the subject matter of Chapter 5 and especially of Chapter 6.

With these issues in mind we may consider the information in Table 2.3, reproduced again from OECD sources. We have already noted the increasingly non-concessional nature of official sector financing and the table indicates as much through the pattern of debt accumulation overall. In 1971 concessional financing was 38 per cent of the total. By 1982–3 the ratio had declined to approximately 22 per cent. As we saw previously (Table A2.2), the reason for this was that although (concessional) ODA had increased substantially over the decade it had been outpaced by official non-concessional finance. Similarly, whereas foreign direct investment had shown a real increase

Table 2.3   *Total disbursed long term debt of developing countries at year-end 1971–83, by source and terms of lending ($ billion)*

Source and terms of lending	1971	1975	1976	1977	1978	1979	1980	1981	1982	1983
1 DAC countries and										
capital markets	68	131	160	200	256	301	342	378	410	445
ODA	24	34	36	41	49	53	57	57	58	60
Total export credits	26	40	49	64	83	98	111	117	124	130
Total private	18	57	74 ·	95	124	150	175	205	228	255
of which Bank										
loans[a]	10	46	59	75	98	123	145	173	194	225
Bonds	4	5	6	9	13	13	15	16	17	15
Other	3	6	9	11	13	14	15	15	16	15
2 Multilateral	9	21	26	32	39	46	55	63	71	79
of which Concessional	6	10	12	14	17	20	24	27	30	33
Total debt	86	173	211	262	331	390	444	497	541	592
of which Concessional	33	59	65	76	88	98	108	114	122	130
Non-concessional	53	114	146	186	243	292	336	383	419	462

Source: OECD (1983), Table H1, p. 213 (abbreviated).
[a] Bank loans other than export credits.

in flow terms per annum it had not kept pace with the rapid growth of private capital market, and especially bank, funding. Thus, OECD data suggests that whereas bank loans represented a little under 12 per cent of total long term debt in 1971, they represented 38 per cent in 1983 despite the somewhat erratic growth already described. Even this understates the importance of overall bank involvement since officially guaranteed export credits require bank finance and we have no figures on the growth of bank short term (less than twelve months) debt. The flow referred to in Table A2.2, however, suggests the importance of this item.

This pattern of accumulated debt therefore reflects the changed nature of the resource flow discussed above. Within the official sector, both bilateral (government to government) and multilateral (e.g. the IBRD) sources became less concessional; that is, rather than carrying a substantial sacrifice by the lender (≥ 25 per cent grant element), loans were increasingly at market-determined rates. On the side of private financing we have seen the increasing relative preponderance of bank lending in contrast with foreign direct investment. Thus, a 'non-debt-creating' flow lost ground to a 'debt-creating' one. What is the significance of the increased reliance on debt?

The fundamental feature of debt finance is that when the debt is incurred, contractual obligations are involved for the borrower in the form of interest and principal repayments. In contrast to the case where financing is by equity (or risk) capital these servicing obligations are independent of the current cash flow being generated by the investment which the loan has financed. The equity holder in contrast receives returns, in the form of dividends, which relate to the current earnings of the enterprise. Given this distinction, the issues raised by Minsky concern the increasing likelihood, in a heavily debt-orientated financial structure, that the cash flow from current operations will be inadequate to cover the contractual service obligations. In these circumstances, when loan principal repayments cannot be met from current receipts, refinancing of debts becomes essential and the viability of the enterprise concerned becomes increasingly dependent on the ability to 'tap' different markets for funds. In Minsky's words, when the existence of the enterprise depends on the ability to refinance its repayment obligations, the system has become dependent on 'speculative' finance. The extreme form of this is where current receipts of the enterprise cannot meet either repayment (of principal) or *interest* obligations. When further borrowing is needed to meet the latter – that is when interest is 'capitalized' – we have Minsky's atmospheric description of 'Ponzi finance'. Clearly, psychological factors for both borrowers and lenders become of central importance in these conditions as relatively minor changes in profitability, or interest rates, cause disproportionate adjustment difficulties.

Returning specifically to international lending we have noted that financial flows to LDCs became proportionately more debt creating on both the official and private sides. Official grant and grant element finance had lost ground to non-concessionary loans and foreign direct (equity) investment had given way to private capital market loan finance. Could this have led to something approximating an international version of the Fisher–Minsky state of overindebtedness? There are certainly interesting parallels but also significant differences.

An initial parallel is the fact, indicated already, that financial innovation, particularly in the form of loan syndications, was an important contributing factor to the growth of LDC indebtedness. It may be argued that these innovations, combined with other factors discussed in Chapter 1, which lowered real interest rates, led to the availability of attractive balance of payments financing. Moreover, although for rather different reasons than those envisaged by Fisher and Minsky, prices in general were tending to rise. In particular, primary commodity prices were relatively strong for much of the period we have been considering. These factors could have combined to increase the perceived 'margins of safety' for borrowers and lenders alike. Dangers multiply, as Minsky points out, when such a combination of circumstances promotes increasing recourse to speculative (refinancing) finance. Quite clearly loan refinancing is an integral part of sovereign lending but, before concluding that overindebtedness on a global scale is threatened, at least one significant factor operating in the other direction must be taken into account.

This factor is the effect of inflation on the debt burden. In the Fisher–Minsky context the debt deflation cycle is triggered when, for Fisher, distress selling lowers the price of capital assets relative to the nominal value of the outstanding debt, and business bankruptcies escalate. Alternatively, for Minsky, rising short term interest rates increase the business cash outflow as it services its debts, and at the same time reduces the discounted present value of future earning streams. These two features, the value of outstanding debt relative to the market value of real assets, and the cost of interest payments relative to cash flow, are critically affected by inflation. An important aspect of inflation is that it blurs the distinction between debt service payments relating to the principal of the loan (or amortization) and those relating to interest. In so far as interest rates rise to reflect the inflation rate expected over the duration of the loan, they increasingly incorporate repayment of principal. A very simple example will make this point clear. In a zero inflation environment a loan of 100 carrying an annual rate of interest of 5 per cent for three years and repayment of principal at the end of the period will have a time profile of returns as follows:

		Year	
	1	2	3
Interest	5	5	5
Principal			100

The net present value will be just 100 at an interest rate of 5 per cent. Since there is no inflation, note that the sums received by the creditors represent 5, 5, and 105 respectively at *today's* prices. If now the annual rate of inflation over the next three years is expected to average 10 per cent, the lender would require compensation in the form of a higher nominal interest rate. The rate that would leave the real return on the loan unchanged would be 15 per cent (the sum of the inflation rate and the initial *real* return), i.e.:

	Year		
	1	2	3
Interest	15	15	15
Principal			100

The real return on the loan is still 5 per cent. However, what do the nominal receipts (payments) in each of the three years represent in terms of today's purchasing power? Prices are now rising at the rate of 10 per cent per year. The value of the receipts shown in terms of today's purchasing power will be (when they accrue):

	Year		
	1	2	3
Value of receipts	13.64	12.4	86.4

When this is compared with the zero inflation returns it is clear that an element of *capital* repayment has been brought forward in time. The interest payments substantially reflect amortization of capital when considered in terms of the purchasing power of today.

This important point suggests that a borrower in these circumstances, with correctly anticipated inflation, would be conducting sound policy in borrowing to cover a significant portion of the interest payments. The basis would be the diminishing value, in real terms, of the original debt. Only if lenders were incorrectly to perceive this debt turnover as speculative (or, worse, Ponzi!) financing, need difficulties arise.

Given such 'front loading' characteristics, the tendency will be for apparent interest payments to rise sharply relative to the level of current output. In the national statistics for borrower nations the problem manifests itself as a somewhat expanded current account deficit, as interest payments are made, and as an associated reduction in national income. What is not being considered is the offsetting capital gain as the real value of outstanding debt declines.

It should be further noted that none of this suggests that creditors or debtors are benefitting from inflation since we have assumed this to be correctly anticipated and therefore reflected in loan rates charged. None the less, a considerable (though diminishing) proportion of LDC debt is still provided at concessional rates and these terms tend to become increasingly 'soft' as inflation rates rise. Two questions therefore arise if we are going to make a realistic assessment of the debt burden and the possibility of overindebtedness. Firstly, how far were the apparently wide current account deficits for LDCs in the 1970s distorted by the early repayment of principal on loans? Secondly, were real interest rates facing LDC borrowers affected by inflation?

These questions will be considered in turn first at the global or broad country group level already employed in this chapter, and then with reference to the major borrowing nations This last focus will then allow us to return to the investment 'shifts' argument first raised in Chapter 1.

For the current account, inflation introduced a distortion by incorporating into the figures an item which should more properly be included in the capital account; the repayment of loan principal. To judge the importance of this item it is necessary to adjust the value of a country's net external liabilities, roughly net foreign indebtedness less foreign exchange reserves which are, of course, also subject to loss of real value. The resulting fall in net indebtedness may then be deducted from the national current account deficit. Table 2.4 gives an indication of the magnitude involved.

In light of those figures, the years over which bank lending were rising in real terms (between 1976 and 1980, cf. Table A2.1) can now be seen against a substantial fall in the value of outstanding indebtedness. This illustrates the point made above in which refinancing of a rising interest burden would be justifiable when seen as early capital repayment. As we have seen, this practice would be acceptable when interest charges fully compensated lenders for the effect of inflation on the value of the debt. How far, in addition, were real interest rates depressed during this period, encouraging further borrowing on world capital markets by LDCs? Two possible influences may be noted here. First, the Sachs argument outlined in Chapter 1, suggested that an increased global propensity to save against diminished investment plans in the OECD nations tended to depress real interest rates, a mechanism not related to inflation.

Table 2.4 *Inflation adjustment for current accounts of non-oil developing countries ($ billions)*

	1973	1974	1975	1976	1977	1978	1979	1980
(1) Current account	−6	−23	−33	−19	−14	−25	−39	−66
(2) Inflation adjusted current account	7	−9	−31	−11	−3	−1	−20	−52
(3) = (2) in $ at 1980 values	15	−15	−49	−17	−5	−2	−22	−52

Source: Stanyer and Whitley (1981).

Notes: (a) Data in row 1 is not identical to data in table 2.1 due to differing country coverage. (b) Data in row 3 provides an estimate of the change in real net external indebtedness.

Table 2.5   *Real interest rates in major industrial countries*

	1965–72	1973–9	Averages 1980	1981	1982
United States	0.7	–0.6	2.33	4.68	4.68
United Kingdom	0.2	–5.4	–4.1	1.13	3.87
Germany	–0.5	–0.6	4.6	7.1	4.0
Japan	0.4	–2.2	8.0	4.84	4.9

Sources: Average data in columns 1 and 2 from Sachs (1981). Annual data for 1980–2 are the author's own calculations representing the annual average difference between treasury bill rates (or call money rates for Germany and Japan), and change in GNP deflator, based on data from the IMF *International Financial Statistics Yearbook 1983.*

Secondly, it is also possible that nominal interest rates may not correct totally for inflation, thus unambiguously benefitting the debtor at the expense of the creditor. This last influence depends on the structure of debt but firstly, how have real interest rates behaved? At the time Sachs was writing, the evidence strongly supported his *a priori* reasoning. However, as Table 2.5 suggests, the post 1979 figures suggest a major reversal.

While it appears to be the case that during the 1970s borrowers benefited from negative real rates of interest, and from declining spreads in the case of sovereign borrowers, both of these trends moved sharply into reverse in the early 1980s. The stance of OECD monetary policy must be seen as a fundamental cause of the high real rates, with particular influence deriving from the USA. How long lasting these influences will be is uncertain but economic policy statements stress the temporary nature of the high real rates prevailing in the developed countries. None the less, in the arguments put forward by Minsky a change in the level of real interest rates evidently witnessed in recent years would suggest mounting difficulty for heavily 'geared' borrowers. Mounting difficulties with debt servicing have become plain in the market crisis of 1982–3 and in the rescheduling problems of 1984. The connection between these difficulties, rising real interest rates and the OECD recession, with its consequences for LDC export market growth, indicates the relevance of another aspect of the Minsky argument.

In the domestic economy context with which he is concerned Minsky argues that financial institutions which have based their growth on short term borrowing (being endangered by rising interest rates) are usually rescued by the intervention of the monetary authorities. The introduction of reserve money creates liquidity for these institutions which would otherwise have been hard pressed to liquidate their asset portfolios. The second type of intervention preventing cumulative decline would be the exercise of government fiscal policy to boost total expenditure. This important intervention helps to prevent the decline of profits which would otherwise lead on to the Fisher deflation process as firms found their debt burden increasingly onerous.

The contrast with the international environment is that no such intervening authority exists on the second level, of fiscal intervention to prevent a fall in 'profits'. Whereas the major international banks would be assisted by inter-governmental co-operation of the Basle agreement type, the ultimate borrower countries cannot look to any body to sustain the demand for their export goods. Moreover, since the bank lending is at floating rates, the risk of rising real interest rates in this instance is passed on to the ultimate borrower.

Just as the impact of inflation on the real burden of external debt could generally be said to have reduced the prospect of overindebtedness, a further qualification must now be entered concerning the adverse impact of rising real interest rates in recent times. At the overall level, the developing countries were somewhat protected from the consequences of rising interest rates by two considerations. First, the fact that a still substantial part of their debt was at fixed interest rates and second in that the bulk of their overseas assets such as foreign exchange reserves were invested at floating rates. OECD data again give an idea of the importance of this distinction, between fixed and floating rates.

Table 2.6 reveals that fixed rate debt, comprising mainly ODA both bilateral and multilateral (including IBRD), bonds and official export credits, adjusted very slowly to the interest rate developments of recent times. As these are nominal rates the real rates on this debt have been negative. Floating interest debt, dominated by bank

Table 2.6 *Average interest rates on fixed and floating rate LDC debt*

		1972/3	1974/6	1977/8	1979	1980	1981	1982	1983
(1)	Fixed interest debt	4.4	4.9	5.5	5.8	6.0	6.0	6.3	6.7
(2)	Floating interest debt	8.3	9.9	8.4	12.3	15.5	17.4	17.3	12.7
(3)	Total debt	5.0	6.0	6.2	7.7	9.0	9.7	10.2	8.7
	of which Low income countries	2.9	3.2	3.4	3.9	3.8	3.8	4.0	3.7
	Lower middle income countries	4.6	5.0	5.2	7.3	8.7	9.0	9.8	8.3
	Upper middle income countries	6.4	7.6	7.8	9.3	11.0	12.1	12.4	10.6

Source: OECD (1983), Table H5, p. 215.

lending, has, on the other hand, been a sensitive barometer of interest rate conditions worldwide. Accordingly, it is, in part, the proportion of a nation's debt made up by these types that determines the severity of impact of rising interest rates. The last three rows of the table illustrate very clearly that the preponderance of floating rate debt rises markedly with the income group of the borrower country. Recall, however, that these rate increases represent an extra burden only if the real rate of interest rises. This would apply to the post 1979 period. Another factor, even for upper middle income countries, is the offset to the interest rates shown in the table provided by the higher returns earned on, for example, foreign exchange reserves.

An earlier OECD (1981, p. 71) study concluded that in 1981 Brazil and Mexico accounted for the 'near totality' of *net* floating interest debt when these offsets were included. At a much lower level, but still positive in net terms, were South Korea, Argentina, Morocco, Philippines and the Ivory Coast.

This brings us, then, to an important conclusion. Given the current account needs of the developing countries in the 1970s it is indebtedness to banks which is most likely to create difficulty. The increasing non-concessionality of ODA will have hurt the lower income LDCs, but since even this finance has been available at modest real interest rates the damage has probably not been severe. It is the fact that bank lending has been heavily concentrated that causes us to focus now on the principal debtors in assessing the manageability of the debt 'problem'. To what extent does overindebtedness apply here? Since we are now concentrating on the major commercial borrowers we can also consider further the extent to which this borrowing might be attributable to an 'investment shift'. In so far as these countries showed a strong investment performance over the period of their accumulating indebtedness, the prospects for the longer term would be much brighter.

Presented in Table 2.7 are individual national data for seven of the ten countries originally studied by Sachs which are also among the top twenty LDC borrowers. The figures presented are for the 1982 value of total debt (long term) and for that attributable to banks.

Of total long term outstanding bank debt, therefore, almost two-thirds is accounted for by these seven countries and as such they represent the bulk of any debt problem. This conclusion would be strengthened if we were to include short term (less than twelve months to maturity) bank debt. Again, these countries have a major share in such finance and it has been an element in the recent debt difficulties of Mexico and Brazil (Amex, 1984). In this context we may consider broad economic performance and the relation of the debt burden to it.

Table 2.8 represents an updated version of the exercise carried out

Table 2.7   *Long term debt of seven developing countries in 1982*
($ billions)

	Total long term debt	of which bank debt
Brazil	72.5	44.5
Mexico	60.5	40.4
Argentina	27.1	15.5
Korea (South)	22.0	8.7
Chile	13.4	8.5
Peru	8.7	2.7
Philippines	12.2	3.9
Percentages of total for LDCs	40%	64%

Source: OECD (1983), Table H6, p. 216.

by Sachs to estimate inflation-adjusted ratios of investment, savings and current account to income.

As already noted, the inflation adjustment in Table 2.8 concerns adding back to GNP the inflationary 'gain' through the decline in real external indebtedness less the equivalent loss in purchasing power of foreign exchange reserves. Investment, savings and the current account are then defined consistent with this adjustment.

Both the savings and the investment ratios reported tend to have a higher value in the second of the two periods (1974–9) for which the data are averaged. While this is not a uniform pattern, the ratios compare quite favourably with those reported by Sachs for the OECD. For fifteen OECD nations the ratios for investment and savings were 0.2 and 0.21 respectively during 1974–9. It is clear, however, that Chile and Peru were not notably successful on these criteria. Although their investment ratios were rising both have had chronic difficulties with debt service. The continuing decline in the Chilean savings ratio in the 1980s is particularly noticeable in this respect. There is some suggestion that a deteriorating savings performance (in 1980) could have had something to do with Brazil's difficulties and both of these countries are subject to more detailed scrutiny in the next chapter.

While available figures terminate too soon to cast light on Mexico's recent difficulties the strong savings and investment performance reported for that country substantially reflects a growing oil export sector. Declining oil prices have been crucial in explaining that country's reversal of fortune.

This rather mixed Latin American experience may be contrasted with the apparently strong performance of the Asian countries reported. Indeed, while there is some support for the Sachs thesis that heavily indebted countries tend also to be those with a rising

Table 2.8 *Inflation adjusted savings–investment performance: selected LDCs*

	Average, 1965–73	Average, 1974–9	1980	1981	1982
Argentina					
I/GNP	0.191	0.245	0.252	0.234	—
S/GNP	0.199	0.25	0.23	0.196	—
CA/GNP	0.001	0.017	–0.027	0.03	—
D/GNP		0.113	0.105	0.197	—
Brazil					
I/GNP	0.216	0.237	0.214	—	—
S/GNP	0.22	0.218	0.179	—	—
CA/GNP	–0.018	–0.034	–0.034	—	—
D/GNP	—	—	0.232	0.23	—
Chile					
I/GNP	0.144	0.117	0.169	0.19	0.147
S/GNP	0.143	1.104	0.154	0.098	0.026
CA/GNP	—	—	–0.056	–0.127	–0.079
D/GNP	—	0.331	0.329	0.37	0.59
Colombia					
I/GNP	0.188	0.194	0.219	—	—
S/GNP	0.174	0.226	0.253	—	—
CA/GNP	–0.03	0.007	0	—	—
D/GNP	—	0.175	0.143	—	—
Mexico					
I/GNP	0.196	0.219	0.243	0.261	—
S/GNP	0.181	0.221	0.267	0.263	—
CA/GNP	–0.027	–0.025	–0.016	–0.032	—
D/GNP	—	—	0.235	0.226	0.352
Peru					
I/GNP	0.128	0.155	0.169	0.192	—
S/GNP	0.146	0.146	0.234	0.187	—
CA/GNP	0.003	–0.023	0.058	–0.024	—
D/GNP	—	—	0.41	0.365	—
Philippines					
I/GNP	0.167	0.23	0.253	0.257	—
S/GNP	0.174	0.251	0.271	0.261	—
CA/GNP	–0.036	–0.04	–0.03	–0.032	—
D/GNP	—	—	0.237	0.256	0.306
Korea (S)					
I/GNP	0.225	0.271	0.32	0.278	0.287
S/GNP	0.174	0.251	0.224	0.222	0.24
CA/GNP	–0.036	–0.04	–0.083	–0.055	–0.021
D/GNP	—	—	0.305	0.308	0.328

Table 2.8 *(cont.)*

	Average, 1965–73	Average, 1974–9	1980	1981	1982
Thailand					
I/GNP	0.223	0.236	0.261	—	—
S/GNP	0.209	0.233	0.251	—	—
CA/GNP	–0.032	–0.025	–0.023	—	—
D/GNP	—	—	0.17	—	—

Source: Average data from Sachs (1981) except for Argentina, Chile and Colombia for which the 1974–9 averages in Sachs were based on incomplete annual data. These were reworked using his methodology. That methodology is fully described in the original and is applied for 1982 and subsequent years, for all countries. Other data are from the IMF's *International Financial Statistics Yearbook 1983.*

Key: I, investment; S, savings; CA, current account; D, outstanding debt as defined by Sachs.

investment performance (as a fraction of GNP), the gap between this and domestic savings has been variable, conducing to variable current account and, therefore, debt accumulation experience. It is this variability of experience which justifies the two case studies to follow.

The inflation-adjusted calculations in Table 2.8 are crude, with, for instance, debts and foreign exchange reserves assumed entirely held in the form of US dollars. Nevertheless, the estimates are consistent with at least two-thirds of reported interest payments reflecting the early repayment of capital. On this basis new borrowing to cover interest payment is not 'Ponzi' finance but an avoidance of the premature repayment of capital.

Despite this consideration and the other more positive aspects of international borrowing considered in this chapter, evidence now suggests a major crisis in international bank lending commencing in 1982. Most tangibly, the crisis manifested itself in a net cash *outflow* from major borrowers back to the international banking system. In other words, 1982 saw the beginning of a net real resource transfer out of the NICs, a situation which cannot be consistent with the long term flow of capital suggested by the investment motive for borrowing outlined in the first chapter, or with the investment shift thesis discussed in the present one.

It is clear that the initial culprit was high world interest rates in 1980–2 which, for several countries, meant that a net outflow of funds commenced before a debt crisis was recognized (Amex, 1984, p. 11). The Amex report, however, stresses that these initial problems were exacerbated by an unwillingness of the banks to 'roll-over' short term debts or to renew maturing medium term debts as they became due.

Evidence for this is contained in the debt data from the World Bank which reveals a decline in outstanding unused credit commitments. In the year to June 1983 these dropped by an estimated $14 billion concentrated in eighteen major borrower nations. The Amex authors suggest three interpretations. First, that banks were reducing available credit lines. Second, that the facilities were being more rapidly drawn down by the borrowers. Thirdly (alternatively), that while the rate of draw down may not have increased, banks were reducing their new commitments. That borrower difficulties were being experienced in the markets is further suggested by the rapid build up of *short term* indebtedness as the new loan commitments were declining.

Evidently, by this time, financial markets were regarding the debt of major borrowers as worrying. Certainly, rates of interest experienced recently would make the position of any debtor more difficult and a short term crisis of confidence of the type we have discussed could be understood.

To what extent, however, have the economic policies of the borrower nations conduced to the crisis? The investment shift argument would be a strong basis for justification of borrowing but our review of the evidence for it has been somewhat inconclusive. While investment spending as a fraction of income seems to have been well maintained, savings performance has been less consistent. These two sides of domestic absorption have helped to explain the current account patterns which have generated the borrowing.

In order to give more consideration to the role of domestic policy in generating debt difficulties, Chapter 3 examines the experience of two debtor countries, Brazil and Chile. That chapter will complete the setting of the scene for the main analysis of risk in the international banking system.

APPENDIX: DEBT COMPOSITION OF CONSTANT VALUES

Table A2.1 Total net resource receipts of developing countries from all sources, 1970–1982 – constant prices ($ billion, 1981 prices)

	1970	1971	1972	1973	1974	1975	1976	1977	1978	1979	1980	1981	1982
I. Official development assistance	21.30	22.18	21.48	24.72	29.10	32.03	30.19	28.82	33.53	33.79	36.21	36.62	34.97
1. Bilateral	18.45	19.03	18.47	20.90	24.13	26.16	24.45	22.18	26.36	27.19	28.65	28.70	27.37
(a) DAC countries	14.58	15.31	14.43	13.80	14.51	14.97	14.09	13.85	15.66	17.28	17.56	18.28	18.93
(b) OPEC countries	1.00	1.07	1.44	3.96	7.32	8.69	7.67	5.88	8.23	7.36	8.47	7.61	5.63
(c) CMEA and other donors	2.86	2.65	2.60	3.14	2.29	2.51	2.69	2.46	2.47	2.54	2.62	2.81	2.81
2. Multilateral agencies	2.86	3.16	3.01	3.82	4.97	5.87	5.74	6.63	7.17	6.60	7.56	7.93	(7.61)
II. Grants by private voluntary agencies	2.22	2.21	2.27	2.67	2.15	2.05	2.00	2.04	1.97	2.06	2.24	2.02	2.36
III. Non-concessional flows	28.22	28.71	29.04	38.71	34.94	52.46	51.77	61.21	69.11	61.08	54.71	69.27	(57.84)
1. Official or officially supported	10.20	11.94	8.19	9.47	13.47	16.10	18.78	21.62	22.92	19.81	21.81	22.14	23.12
(a) Private export credits (DAC)	5.39	6.58	3.14	2.26	4.23	6.76	10.00	12.14	11.58	9.37	10.79	11.33	(9.19)
(b) Official export credits (DAC)	1.52	1.75	1.62	2.20	1.41	1.83	2.06	1.98	2.65	1.83	2.39	2.01	(2.50)
(c) Multilateral	1.83	2.23	2.21	2.55	3.19	3.87	3.77	3.70	3.68	4.40	4.70	5.68	6.82
(d) Other official and private flows (DAC)	0.64	0.68	0.98	1.99	1.46	1.15	1.19	0.86	1.62	1.21	2.17	1.96	(3.07)
(e) Other donors	0.82	0.70	0.24	0.47	3.18	2.49	1.76	2.94	3.39	3.01	1.77	1.16	(1.53)
2. Private	18.01	16.77	20.86	29.24	21.46	36.36	32.98	39.59	46.18	41.27	32.90	47.13	34.73
(a) Direct investment	9.51	8.03	9.24	9.20	3.33	17.37	12.33	13.49	13.83	14.20	10.22	16.13	(11.24)
(b) Bank sector	7.73	8.01	10.48	18.91	17.64	18.35	18.84	21.70	27.68	26.35	21.34	29.00	(21.45)
(c) Bond lending	0.77	0.73	1.14	1.13	0.49	0.64	1.81	4.40	4.67	0.72	1.34	2.00	2.04
Total receipts (I+II+III)	51.75	53.11	52.79	66.10	66.19	86.54	83.96	92.07	104.61	96.93	93.16	107.92	95.18

Source: OECD (1983), Table III.2.
Note: Row III excludes bond lending and row III.2 (b) excludes bank-financed private export credits displayed separately under line III.1 (a).

Table A2.2   Components in the increase in resource transfers 1970–82 (real terms: 1981 prices and exchange rates)

	1970		1982		Increase ($b)	Percentage of increase (%)	Increase in each component (%)
	$b	Percentage of total (%)	$b	Percentage of total (%)			
Total	51	100	98	100	47	100	92
I. ODA	21	41	35	36	14	30	67
DAC (bilateral)	15	29	18	18	3	6	20
OPEC (bilateral)	1	2	6	6	5	11	500
Other donors	2	4	3	3	1	2	50
Multilateral	3	6	8	8	5	11	167
II. Private grants	2	4	2	2	0	0	0
III. Non-concessional	28	55	61	62	33	70	118
(a) Private							
Direct investment	10	20	14	14	4	9	40
Capital market finance (bank sector + bonds)	8	16	23	23	15	32	188
(b) Official or officially-supported							
Export credits (DAC)	7	14	12	12	5	11	71
Other	1	2	5	5	4	9	400
(c) Multilateral	2	4	7	7	5	11	250

Source: OECD (1983), Table III.3.

3 Outward-looking policies in an inward-looking world: the cases of Brazil and Chile

It was argued in the previous chapter that the distribution of indebtedness between countries, particularly within the Third World, could not be explained by relative oil dependence. Investment performance, in relation to domestic savings behaviour, has been a significant element in determining the distribution. Emerging from this finding is the conclusion that a proper understanding of recent debt history requires consideration of the policies followed by individual borrowing countries.

Investment performance undoubtedly has contributed substantially to the debts accumulated by Brazil and Mexico. As the two largest debtors it is an interesting indication that they also experienced, between 1972 and 1981, a relatively rapid accumulation in their territories of the stock of American-owned direct investment. Data on the book value of American-owned enterprises, on an annual year end basis are available in various issues of the US Department of Commerce publication: *Survey of Current Business*. With reference to the investment shifts argument reviewed in the previous chapter, the growth in the nominal dollar stock of American foreign direct investment in all countries was 8.86 per cent between 1972 and 1981. For the developed 'host' countries the value was 8 per cent whereas for developing countries the rate of growth was 10.5 per cent. These figures cover all types of enterprise and, on the basis of 1981 figures, Brazil and Mexico together accounted for 27 per cent of *the total* stocks of US direct investment in LDCs. For manufacturing investments alone, however, the share of the two countries was almost 55 per cent. The nominal dollar growth of the stock between 1972 and 1981 was between 12 per cent and 13 per cent in both countries for all categories *and* for manufacturing alone.[1]

While American-owned foreign investment is only a part of the total, and there are obvious geographic reasons for American-owned firms to choose Mexico as a 'foreign' base for their re-exports to the

United States, the figures quoted do suggest that there were strong inducements to invest in Brazil and Mexico during the 1970s. To this extent, at least for these two major debtors, concentration of debt has to some extent been matched by concentration of American-owned manufacturing investment. Indeed one estimate for Brazil suggests that between the end of 1973 and 1979 the stock of *total* direct foreign investment (from all sources) grew at an annual average rate of 23 per cent, which would be similar to the growth of gross debt in that period (Diaz-Alejandro, 1983).

Although for Brazil and Mexico strong inducements to invest must have been a significant part of the explanation of debt accumulation, investment behaviour must be compared with the generation of domestic savings for a more complete understanding, and this links directly to domestic economic policy. In the case of Mexico, for instance, despite the considerable oil revenues being projected at the time (and accounting for two-thirds of merchandise exports in 1980), concern was being expressed at the extent to which Mexico was finding it necessary to borrow abroad. A failure to generate domestic savings, or at least to prevent their leakage overseas, were proximate causes of this 'excess' borrowing (Solomon, 1981).

Despite Mexico's obvious importance, her status as a major oil exporter perhaps diminishes the generality of her experience. Her economic policies also, probably due to excessive oil-based optimism, have been highly variable. In this chapter, therefore, we focus on the emergence of debt problems in Brazil and Chile. Brazil, as a diversified economy with the second largest debt accumulation after Mexico, is an obvious choice. Chile, however, shares with Brazil some common experiences, in particular the pursuit of a systematic domestic economic policy aimed at stabilization in the context of high inflation. A rapidly growing literature on the impact of stabilization programmes, particularly those supported by the IMF, emphasizes the importance of international financial flows. It is in these cases, especially, that the link between debt accumulation and domestic economic strategy becomes especially interesting. An additional important reason for discussing these countries together is that they have both sought to shift the emphasis of their general economic policies away from the, so called, 'inward looking' import substitution-based development strategy. With its original justification going back to World War II, increasing disillusion with the consequences has led to considerable academic support for more 'outward looking', export-oriented programmes. In varying degrees these countries have tried to move away from trade restriction to trade promotion. How have these important issues related to the growth of debt?

BRAZIL

In common with other developing countries and, in particular, with other Latin American republics, Brazil's post-war development was characterized by industrialization focused on the evolution of the home market (e.g. Baer, 1972). The practice of protecting emergent domestic industries from foreign competition by the imposition of tariffs together with the combination of a pegged exchange rate and high domestic inflation led to major distortion of the price mechanism. While tariffs translated into high (though variable) *effective* protection of manufacturing value added (essentially wages and profits), an increasingly overvalued exchange rate discouraged traditional agricultural and newer export sectors (cf. Bergsman, 1970).

Despite the increasing severity of these distortions the Brazilian economy in the post-war period to 1961 grew at an average annual rate of around 7 per cent. The reversal of this favourable experience occurred in 1962–3 when annual growth rates declined markedly. These economic reverses, with the apparent loss of momentum of industrial expansion, contributed to the military coup in April 1964. Since that date Brazil has been ruled by successive military regimes which have supported, and were able to impose, significant shifts in economic policy. The first three years were characterized by economic austerity aimed at reducing a rate of inflation which touched 140 per cent as an annual rate in early 1964.

In March 1967 a new (military) president appointed a team of economic advisers under the leadership of Delfim Netto, the Finance Minister, committed to continuing financial stabilization, public sector retrenchment and a revival of private sector investment and growth. Although seen as a 'gradualist' programme for reducing inflation (given substantial cost-push elements in the Brazilian context), explicit attention was given to the need to reduce distortions in the price mechanism. The 1964–7 period of the first government was dominated by concern for economic stabilization. Foreign debts accumulated from earlier balance of payments deficits necessitated collaboration with the IMF and decelerating monetary growth targets, together with reduced public sector deficits, were the core of policy in those years.

Despite the initial short term focus, other reforms took place which marked the beginning of a fundamental shift in the orientation of economic policy. Orientation towards exports as a leading sector, away from import substitution, manifested itself in a cumulative devaluation of the cruzeiro against the dollar of 55 per cent between early 1964 and 1967. Although this did not succeed in reflecting fully the differential Brazilian inflation of the time, the intention had been that it should do so and a series of fiscal and credit measures to boost exports were initiated.

While these attempts were being made to ensure that the price mechanism reflected the true value of earning foreign exchange, a start was made in reforming credit markets. Massive distortions had arisen here with traditional usury laws contributing to the maintenance of negative real rates of interest. This penalty on financial savings was becoming more severe as inflation accelerated up to 1964 with the predictable consequence that consumption and real estate 'investments' were encouraged. From the point of view of borrowers, the major firms with access to the rationed credit supplies became heavily 'over-geared'. This rational response to a negative real interest rate on borrowed funds was later to render these firms prone to bankruptcy as monetary correction, first applied to the return on government bonds in 1964, was allowed for private debt in 1966. This correction for inflation conduced to the emergence of positive *real* rates of interest for the first time in 1966.

The monetary correction measure had been explicitly intended to stimulate private savings. The government was able to raise substantial revenues by means of readjustable treasury bonds (ORTN), especially after an adjustment for inflation based on exchange rate depreciation was allowed. At the same time the demand for bank savings deposits increased.

All of these measures concerning the exchange rate, export promotion and credit market reform were to be further developed in a systematic way by the economic planners appointed under the second (military) president in 1967. The key development announced in August 1968 by Finance Minister Netto was of a 'crawling peg' exchange rate regime. The fixed exchange rate under this arrangement, sometimes known as the 'trotting peg' in the Brazilian context, is devalued by small amounts at frequent intervals in order to reflect on-going differential inflation between Brazil and her trading partners. Typical adjustment would be of 1.5 per cent over roughly forty days, amounts sufficiently small, when taking into account interest differentials and brokerage costs, to prevent speculative flight of funds in anticipation of the devaluation. By and large this system has permitted the Brazilian trade sector to maintain its competitiveness in the face of high domestic inflation.

Fiscal and other incentives to exporting were further developed after 1967 and in March of that year efforts at liberalizing imports over the previous three years culminated in a reduction of the tariff structure. The rationale for this at the time was that the deflationary period of 1964–7 led to a substantial decline in imports and a current account surplus. In order to avoid involuntary Brazilian net investment abroad as a consequence of the trade surplus a rise in imports was justifiable.

In contrast to this systematic 'opening' of the economy, interest rate policy was somewhat more eclectic. Concern that high domestic interest rates were promoting cost-push inflation pressures led to attempts to use subsidies to the banking sector in order to bring rates down. Unfortunately, the banking sector was not characterized by competitive behaviour and the scheme had little success. More significantly, following the implementation of Resolution 63 in 1966, Brazilian firms were increasingly able to tap foreign credit markets as commercial and investment banks were allowed to intermediate between the firms (which were usually unknown abroad) and the foreign capital markets. This measure did have a beneficial effect in bringing loan rates down nearer to institutional borrowing rates at home and abroad.

General recourse to foreign financial markets was of increasing importance by the early 1970s to finance Brazil's trade deficit (which emerged in 1967). A part of these inflows was the result of a return flow of Brazilian capital attracted by the new exchange rate arrangements and the high domestic interest rates. Although Brazil had a debt service ratio (interest plus amortization payments as a percentage of exports) of about 36 per cent by 1972, commentators at the time did not see this as any threat to continued economic growth (e.g. Syvrud, 1974, p. 209).

This assessment turned out to be amply justified for, despite the 1973–4 oil crisis, Brazil managed to sustain an impressive growth of her real GNP through the 1970s. Running at 12 per cent per annum between 1971 and 1973, it sustained 8 per cent in 1974–6 and nearly 6 per cent in 1977–9 (Diaz-Alejandro, 1983).

As Diaz-Alejandro points out, although inflation accelerated after 1973, and there were large current account deficits between 1974 and 1979, the growth rate of exernal debt was not far above that of merchandise exports. When it is recognized that Brazil experienced a 20 per cent decline in the terms of trade over 1974–5, and that roughly half of the huge increase in her import bill over the 1972–3 level was the result of higher prices, this increased indebtedness does not appear excessive. It was contained, after 1974–5, by continuing export success and the suppression of imports by tariff increases and other restrictions.

On the debit side, however, the public sector became increasingly important in sustaining domestic economic activity. One method was the use of interest rate subsidies on credit progammes administered through the Central Bank and the Bank of Brazil (IBRD, 1981, p. 70). The rates charged became increasingly negative in real terms and financial savings decelerated. Foreign borrowing reflected increased reliance on foreign savings to sustain a high rate of investment spending (IBRD, 1981). It should be emphasized, however, that Brazil *was* spending substantially on investment and although the efficiency of some of these projects was questionable (e.g. the 'gasohol' programme), real interest rates on international capital markets were low, making even marginal projects worthwhile. In this way, the mechanism stressed by Sachs to which we have referred appears to be supported in the Brazilian context.

If, on the other hand, a crisis of 'overindebtedness' can be identified, it would be from 1979–80. The difficulties which arose in the 1980s can most usefully be assessed by direct reference to Diaz-Alejandro's 'counter-factual' analysis of the situation facing Brazilian planners following the announcement of the second oil price increase in 1979. The counter-factual position is built on plausible assumptions of what could have been known by planners in 1979. A potential growth of the dollar value of exports, and other current and capital account items, is combined with a predetermined growth of external borrowing. These together determine the *ex ante* permissible growth of imports. Assumptions about import prices are then invoked to derive from import values the implications for import volume. On the basis of a highly conservative growth of debt, with net debt expanding at the expected international interest rate so as merely to prevent a net resource outflow, the conclusions of the analysis are troubling. Imports would have had to be compressed by a very substantial real devaluation.

In comparing the counter-factual with the actual out-turn a number of important conclusions are evident. While exports fare better in dollar values than might have been expected during 1980–1, there is a sharp reverse in 1982 when the value of merchandise exports declined. Interestingly, much of this can be put down to the collapse of Brazil's newly found export markets in the rest of Latin America and the Third World. As Diaz-Alejandro points out, this collapse is in part attributable to the growing debt difficulties of these other developing countries and to the collapse of *their* export earnings.

On the other side of the accounts, terms of trade losses from imports are more severe than reasonable predictions in 1980 and 1981. This combination of circumstances on the export and import side led to policies producing a reduction of real GNP in 1981 and growth in 1982 which would mean a further fall in *per capita* income. Imports were severely restricted and fell both absolutely and below that which the 'prudent planner' in 1979 might have allowed. An analysis of the recessionary policies self-administered by the Brazilian authorities in 1981 in the face of the export–import trends has been provided by

Dornbusch (1982), who emphasizes the peculiar features of inflation in the Brazilian context. As the government seeks to finance public sector deficits by non-inflationary borrowing from the private sector, the stock of government debt (treasury bonds, etc.) increases, suggesting the need for higher interest rates to clear the issue. Moreover, a policy of accelerating the downward crawl of the pegged exchange rate (which occurred) *increases* the attractiveness of foreign securities compared with locally issued ones of the type mentioned. This further influence driving up local interest rates massively 'crowds out' private investment spending. Even if the devaluation is successful in raising exports, it also contributes, especially through wage indexation to rising inflation. These circumstances are sufficient to generate severe 'stagflation' with rapid price increases, declining real income and high real rates of interest.

The reality for Brazil in 1981 was for real output to contract for the first time in thirty years (industrial production declining by 9.3 per cent) against a background of interest rates 25–30 per cent above the rate of inflation (Economist, 1982, p. 55).

In addition to this domestic misery endured to maintain international creditworthiness in the face of terms of trade losses of 'Great Depression' proportions, interest rates on existing foreign borrowings began to escalate alarmingly. Indeed, the bulk of the excess of debt service payments over the conservative projections of the 'prudent planner' in 1979 are due to rising world interest rates rather than a higher level of debt (Diaz-Alejandro, 1983, pp. 524–6).

On the basis of this very sketchy review of Brazilian experience since 1967 it is difficult to avoid the impression that something of the Fisher–Minsky overindebtedness thesis applies in this case to international debt. During the 'boom' years to 1979 the evidence strongly favours seeing Brazil as a rapidly growing country where rising net foreign debt in substantial part reflected the burgeoning opportunities for investment. Certainly until 1979–80 little concern was expressed that Brazilian debt was excessive. Low world interest rates amply justified recourse to these external funds. After 1979, however, a debt sustainable in one set of circumstances became difficult to sustain in another. Terms of trade losses and rising world interest rates overturned all reasonable calculations producing a crisis of confidence among lenders.

Recently assembled evidence suggests that this crisis of confidence emerged first in 1979. There was a marked reduction in unused credit commitments made by lenders to Brazil *simultaneously* with the jump in oil payments needs (Amex, 1984, p. 56). By 1982, Brazil's position in world markets was deteriorating further as indicated by a rapid build up of short term debt. This in turn suggests an unwillingness to make medium term commitments on the part of lenders and a rapidly deteriorating situation led to the debt rescheduling of 1982 under IMF auspices.

Given the emergence of these circumstances, what are the prospects for a resumption of expansion in Brazil? The recent retrenchment for the domestic economy has been severe indeed with the current IMF-inspired programme suggesting zero growth again for 1984. One estimate suggests that even on growth for the world economy along the most optimistic of IMF projections, Brazil can expect no per capita income growth until 1987–8 (Kaletsky, 1984). How are such projections derived and how sensitive are they to various assumptions?

A number of debt projection models have been offered in the literature, but one which most closely reflects World Bank thinking regards the growth of net borrowing (net loans minus debt servicing) as financing the gap between projected imports and exports given a certain growth path for the economy (Feder, 1980). The rate of investment spending is determined by this growth path and a given incremental capital : output ratio. Clearly net borrowing also finances the gap between investment spending and domestic savings but these 'two gaps' need not always be equal *ex ante*. What is clear, however, is that the evolution of indebtedness will be crucially determined by the development of domestic savings *vis à vis* investment. If, for instance, marginal savings increase by more than the required increment of investment, net borrowing can decline with growth (Feder, 1980, p. 355).

Such a highly simplified model cannot seriously be used for purposes of 'forecasting' how indebtedness will grow. The official World Bank model, for instance, disaggregates and estimates prospects for imports and exports whereas the model used here merely assumes an export growth rate. Similarly the simple model does not differentiate the planned development of output supply from the expected development of aggregate demand in the economy; the latter is assumed to be planned. The World Bank model does make this distinction.

None the less the basic features of the model help to highlight critical features of debt accumulation starting from the contemporary position of our chosen countries. The values chosen from the parameters in the model are displayed in Table 3.1. The initial total indebtedness (D = \$93 billion) is the latest 'market' estimate quoted in Amex (1984, p. 30), as is the implicit interest rate (i) for 1982 (Amex, 1984, Table 6, p. 61). The amortization ratio (a) in turn uses the Amex estimate of debt service payments allowing for 'excess' short term debt. This important consideration concerns the inadequacy of the standard (medium term) debt service payments when 1982–3

Table 3.1   *Brazil: debt service:export ratio projections*

Assumptions
$D = \$93$ billion; $i = 0.109$; $K = 2.53$; $s = 0.162$; $g = 0.08$; $a = 0.102$; $e = 0.11$

Unchanged interest rates on external debt
Peak ratio = 1.079 reached in 1988–9; the ratio both climbing and falling slowly to and from those years

On IMF interest rates projections
Peak ratio = 1.052 reached in 1985; the ratio falls quickly after that year

witnessed a massive increase in short term borrowing as credit markets contracted. The Amex debt service figure therefore includes medium term debt service (interest plus principal), short term interest and the 'excess' of short term debt principal repayment. The excess is measured over the short term debt which would be required to finance six months' imports. As trade finance arises more or less automatically with the flow of imports it would be necessary to exclude them from any assessment of debt servicing burden. The amortization ratio is calculated by deducting from the debt service payments just defined the interest payment component.

The marginal savings rate (s) used reflects the performance of the Brazilian economy between 1966 and 1980, over which total consumption was regressed on income and time (using the identity 1 − mpc = mps). Similarly, the incremental capital : output ratio (K) is derived over the same period by dividing the average share of investment (gross fixed capital formation) in GDP by the trend rate of growth of the latter in real terms.

The final required values concern assumptions about the *future* rate of growth of income (g) and the rate of growth of export earnings (e). To be consistent with the calculation of interest and amortization payments in dollar terms both income and export growth rates incorporate the *world* rate of price inflation used most recently by the IMF (1984, p. 157). This value of 4 per cent is added to an assumed underlying very small improvement in income per capita and reflects the gloomy predictions mentioned earlier rather than Brazil's successful performance to 1980. For export *volume* growth the IMF 'base scenario' for the growth of manufactured exports of roughly 7 per cent is taken (IMF, 1984, p. 71), implying an 11 per cent growth of dollar receipts. The terms of trade are assumed unchanged.

Two simulations for Brazil's debt service : export ratio are reported.

The first is based on present interest rates remaining unchanged and the second assumes the IMF 'base scenario' projection, (IMF, 1984, p. 158). These postulate a 2 percentage point reduction from present levels during 1986–7 and a further 1 percentage point reduction for 1988–90 inclusive.

Given slow income growth, reasonably rapid growth of export earnings and continuing success in maintaining the productivity of new investment, (reflected in K), nothing in the above figures suggests that Brazil would be unable to maintain the debt service payments implied. Although the rate is high by international standards it is little different from the value faced by Brazil today.

Nevertheless, at current interest rates, Brazil faces years of relative stagnation to prevent the debt service ratio from rising. Only if international interest rates begin to fall does some freedom for manoeuvre emerge, as the IMF interest rate projection-based simulation suggests. The 'knife edge' nature of the problem is highlighted when either a fall in the rate of growth of export earnings or a diminution in the productivity of new investment (a rise in K) is contemplated. For either event the debt service ratio would rise substantially to untenable levels.

Even on the assumptions used a further point needs to be made. With income growing slower than export earnings the ratio of outstanding debt to income rises *continuously* from present levels (although this occurs slowly). An improvement in domestic savings performance is required to prevent this undesirable (for borrower and lender) outcome. A value of $s = 0.185$ would be sufficient to make the debt : income ratio *decline* continuously given the above assumptions and unchanged interest rates. In turn, an improvement in the domestic savings rate would create room for more growth while avoiding a rise in the debt service ratio. Clearly, domestic savings performance becomes a key issue for any given external circumstances, and even the higher value for s mentioned is low by the standards of other NICs (cf. Feder, 1980, p. 357). Furthermore, a rise in the savings ratio would be especially called for should the productivity of new investment begin to decline from the value for K which has been assumed on the basis of successful past performance.

In fact, while our projections have shown the importance of certain critical variables in determining the profile of debt service payments, it is clear that they are over optimistic. Between 1980 and 1983 per capita GDP was in fact declining at an average rate of 4.1 per cent per year, with further decline anticipated; contrary to the (small) growth implied by our projections. Two critical values appear to have been involved in the current depression. First, export growth in dollar terms only achieved 7 per cent per annum in the early 1980s while the effective interest rate on Brazil's debt, allowing for fees and risk premia, has been estimated at around 13 per cent. Such values in the projection exercise display untenable debt service ratios and the result has been the decline in activity so far witnessed in the 1980s. While over simplistic the current crisis may be seen at least partly as being 'triggered' by the deterioration of external conditions indicated by these two statistics. There is indeed some self-fulfilment about the result since it is in part the risk premia incorporated in the interest rates paid by Brazil which have generated the crisis in debt service ratios (Dornbusch, 1983, p. 549). Again, the 'overindebtedness' thesis seems to have some relevance in this context.

CHILE

Whereas the early reforms pursued by the Brazilian military authorities were 'gradualist' in their aim of financial stabilization and price reform, the military coup in Chile in 1973 was followed by dramatic policy shifts. As in the previous case the explicit intention was to stabilize the economy in the short term, while aiming at considerable structural change in the medium term. The more hurried application of the policy changes could be seen as a consequence of the financial inheritance of the new regime. Under the Popular Unity government of Salvador Allende social programmes, especially subsidies, were being financed by monetary expansion. A fiscal deficit of around 30 per cent of GNP could only be financed in this way in the absence of a substantial capital market, so that by September 1973 inflation was running at 400 per cent per annum.

Extreme distortions of prices across all markets, largely due to government intervention, persuaded the new regime to abolish most price controls within a few days of the coup. The close relationship between fiscal deficits through monetary expansion and hyperinflation provided the reason for the precipitate reduction of government spending. Government investment diminished (as a fraction of GNP) by more than half between 1970 and 1979. Public expenditure in other areas was reduced while proportions were shifted in favour of social programmes such as education and housing. Even here, however, *real per capita* expenditure declined.

The reduction of public spending, initially on subsidies, together with major taxation reform (in the direction of value added tax and away from upper income and wealth taxes) and a successful attempt to improve collection brought the fiscal deficit down to 2.5 per cent of

GDP by 1975. In consequence, severely restrictive monetary policy was able to commence in 1974 although this did not, as expected, produce an immediate decline in inflation. The removal of price controls, already mentioned, together with the fact that data on the reduction of the money supply were in arrears by several months, actually caused inflation to accelerate. The main reason was the impact of the higher prices on the consumer price index which was itself the immediate yardstick used in price setting by businessmen.

The initial impact of all this was a substantial reduction of economic activity. Thus, during 1975 industrial production fell by 28 per cent and GDP by 13 per cent. Real wages, on the other hand, fell by about 40 per cent during that year through curtailment of trade union activity and other deliberate policy initiatives. Inflation remained at around 300 per cent on an annual basis, however, and this led to a significant reinforcement of the counter-inflation strategy involving the active use of the exchange rate.

Before dealing with the important issue of the exchange rate policy and international borrowing, we should note that the exchange rate policy to support counter-inflation strategy was somewhat at variance with its supposed role in another important area of the regime's concerns. This involved the more medium term issue of altering the economic structure of the country.

The Allende government had accentuated the policies of previous administrations which had had the effect of massively restricting economic relationships between Chile and the rest of the world. One writer has argued that Chile had one of the world's most protected economies, with tariff rates as high as 800 per cent and a modal value of around 100 per cent. These explicit tariffs were supported by other trade barriers, such as prior deposits, all with the intention of stimulating import substitution-based industrialization (Sjaastad, 1984).

Interestingly, the longer term intention of turning the economy 'outward', towards export-led growth, of enhancing the role of the private sector and of withdrawing the state from the economic arena arguably had priority over reducing inflation (Foxley, 1982). Accordingly, from tariffs of the level mentioned in 1973, gradual reductions culminated in the announcement of a uniform 10 per cent tariff, excluding vehicles, in June 1979.

The initial intention had been to maintain an exchange rate favourable to Chilean exports while lower tariffs reduced the costs of intermediate inputs for Chilean industrialists. Again, as the volume of imports increased it was expected that the exchange rate would depreciate and further promote exports. Difficulties with the counter-inflation strategy to mid 1976, however, led to the decision to supplement monetary control with a *reduced* rate of depreciation of the peso. Indeed in June 1976 and March 1977 exchange rate *revaluations* were made on the argument that, by reducing the local currency price increases on imported goods, domestic prices would begin to reflect international levels. This policy was highly successful, given its intentions, for shortly after the second revaluation inflation declined to 50 per cent at an annual rate. This anti-inflationary use of the exchange rate continued from December 1977 with a pre-announced table of (declining) rates of devaluation and culminated with the return to fixed exchange rates in 1979. Given the domestic rates of inflation experienced, these exchange rate interventions led to substantial real appreciation of the peso between 1977 and 1981.

The conflict between the exchange rate needed to promote export growth (and 'viable' import substitution) on the one hand and to promote convergence to global inflation rates on the other finally reached crisis in the second half of 1982. When the exchange rate was fixed in 1979, inflation in Chile was running at 30 per cent compared with a 'world' rate of roughly 12 per cent. It took eighteen months for these rates to converge and the current account of the balance of payments deteriorated markedly in 1981. Monetary contraction was initially invoked to deal with the payments deficit, the latter helping to bring about the former, with dramatic recessionary consequences. The peso was finally devalued between July 1982 and February 1983 by 95 per cent.

After 1978, the exchange rate as a counter-inflation weapon was conducing to a widening trade deficit which, in turn, had to be financed by capital inflows. Certain aspects of this capital inflow are of direct interest in the present context and need to be related to another feature of the domestic economic reforms embarked upon by the military regime. In complete contrast to the situation prevailing in late 1973, where the commercial banks had mainly been taken into state ownership, most were back in private sector hands by the end of 1975. New non-bank financial institutions were permitted, from 1974, to compete for resources at a freely determined rate of interest. This permitted the new institutions to grow at the expense of the privatized banks since a legal maximum interest rate for the latter remained in force until April 1975. The gradual decontrol of interest rates was supported, again during 1975, with the removal of various quantitative restrictions on bank lending. These reforms, of course, were in the spirit of the appeal to market forces in resource allocation. Both financial savings and the efficient allocation of investable funds were expected to be promoted by the new system.

Unfortunately, the impact of these reforms, in the economic conditions facing Chile at the time, was perverse. With high inflation (and the associated climate of expectations), together with high reserve requirements continuing to act as a 'tax' on financial intermediation, the *real* rate facing borrowers has been estimated as reaching 75 per cent in 1975 and 1976 (Sjaastad, 1984, p. 11). The real rates for depositors, however, remained around zero, indicating both the 'tax' effects referred to and, presumably, a continuing failure of competition in the banking system.

The mechanism behind these perverse results relies heavily on the 'institutional' nature of the inflation process in Chile, as in other Latin American republics. Monetary contraction and a policy of disinflationary exchange rate management such as that followed from 1976 could not bring forth an *immediate* proportionate reduction in the *rate* of inflation. Two consequences were that the domestic and foreign competitiveness of domestic producers declined (despite reduced input costs) *vis-à-vis* import prices, and the squeeze on the real money supply raised interest rates substantially especially as the stock of government bonds continued to rise, albeit more slowly (Dornbusch, 1982). Lingering inflationary expectations on the part of savers would help to 'justify' the rates of interest observed, providing another example of 'inertia' in the inflation process (McKinnon, 1980).

These high (real) interest rates, together with the new policy of administered exchange rates, were highly conducive to the inflow of capital from abroad. As long as interest rates were sufficient to offset the risk that exchange rate policy would be thrown into reverse by enforced devaluation of the peso the capital flow continued and sustained the burgeoning trade deficit.

Interestingly, in the Chilean example, the rate of interest necessary to produce a rise in domestic savings, e.g. growth of bank time deposits, appears to have been higher than the rate required by holders of financial capital abroad to compensate them for the risks of peso devaluation (McKinnon, 1980, p. 32). Both repatriated Chilean capital and borrowings from the international banking system became increasingly attractive sources of finance with domestic deposit rates in 1980 and 1981 being 20 percentage points above the London inter-bank offer rate (LIBOR) (Sjaastad, 1984). This discrepancy between the cost of internally generated finance and foreign borrowing rates can partly be explained by lingering restrictions on access to foreign borrowing. Thus for Chilean institutions foreign borrowing was limited to a set percentage of the value of assets (Foxley, 1982), and arbitrage by banks in foreign transactions was also restricted. None the less, for institutions with some access to foreign borrowing, the profitability of domestic business so financed was high. Perhaps not surprisingly about 50 per cent of Chilean foreign borrowing was channelled through Chilean banks, a lot of this being on behalf of the private sector and not guaranteed by the Chilean authorities (Amex, 1984, p. 72). Such arrangements, of course, cannot be sustained indefinitely and foreign inflows faltered as the balance of payments current account continued to deteriorate during 1981. As already mentioned, the devaluations occurred during 1982 and 1983.

With the combination of circumstances and policies just reviewed it is difficult to believe that Chile conforms as closely as Brazil to the investment shifts view of the determination of her international debt. The foreign funds appear to have financed a considerable increase in the concentration of ownership of *existing* assets in the first instance. Thus, such loans have financed the 'privatization' of enterprises formerly in the government sector. While raising government revenues, investment spending by the latter has been reduced and reliance on the private sector for future economic growth has been made very clear. Unfortunately, but not surprisingly given our discussion of real interest rates, private investment spending has been weak by historical standards. As a ratio to GDP, investment spending averaged 15.3 per cent in the decade 1960–70. Between 1970 and 1979 it was 11.7 per cent and slightly less in the last five years of that period (Foxley, 1982, Table 2). The overall success or failure of the Chilean 'monetarist' experiment remains intensely controversial, with the weaknesses mentioned being offset in some eyes by the massive reduction in inflation and a highly impressive growth of non-traditional exports. Mineral exports declined as a share of total exports from around 69 per cent in 1975 to 59 per cent by 1982. The share of both agricultural and industrial products increased, from 5.6 to 9.8 per cent and from 25.2 to 30.9 per cent respectively. (Sjaastad, 1984, Table 4). The economy enjoyed a rapid recovery of activity between 1976 and 1981 in an environment of *declining* inflation, real growth averaging 7 per cent per annum.

From our own point of view, however, it is the *sustainability* of this, briefly, improved economic performance that is crucial, and questionable in view of the low level of investment spending. What is certainly true is that while imports of consumer goods increased dramatically between 1975 and 1982 the share of capital goods in total imports declined very markedly (Sjaastad, 1984, Table 3). The least favourable interpretation of the Chilean foreign borrowing experience would be that it has helped to fuel a concentration in the ownership of existing resources in favour of the already privileged sections of society, while also financing consumption spending by these groups on imported durables.

Such an interpretation would be highly disquieting for those who have lent money to Chile and the question now arises as to the ability

Table 3.2   *Chile: debt service:export ratio projections*

Assumptions
$D=\$17.9$ billion; $i=0.1$; $K=3.892$; $s=0.174$; $g=0.08$; $a=0.1234$; $e=0.11$

Unchanged interest rates on external debt
Ratio rises to 1.83 in 1992, declining slowly thereafter

On IMF interest rate projections
Peak ratio of 1.54 reached in 1985, falls as projected interest rate reductions occur, but *trend* only downwards after 1991 when the ratio declines slowly from 1.39

of that country to service the debts accumulated. To examine this issue we may return to the projection model used earlier for Brazil. Using the same sources and procedures as in the earlier case study (with s and K based on the period 1973–82), we report the comparable simulations for Chile in Table 3.2.

In these projections from current levels of debt, Chile suffers from an incremental capital : output ratio (K) significantly higher than that of Brazil but not excessively high by international standards. Other ratio values are of a similar order. On these assumptions, the first projection indicates mounting difficulties, leading to historically untenable debt service in relation to exports. Even on the assumption of falling interest rates the values for the ratio appear excessive and unsustainable.

A substantial revision could be achieved at a stroke by an improvement in the world price of copper, still heavily represented (between 40 and 50 per cent) in merchandise exports. Even given this, however, real growth of output would continually be threatened with debt service difficulties. Again, these simulations are illustrative and are not intended seriously as projections. Once more they are counter-factual; Chile has experienced deep recession since 1982, but it could be argued that the simulations give some insight into the causes of the recession.

In some respects it is surprising that Chile should have found itself in such crisis in 1982–3 after following policies broadly supported by the international financial community. The best hope for improvement would seem to be a revival of world copper prices together with a substantial improvement in the domestic savings ratio (s). Some of the reforms described have been intended to contribute to this end and it may be that the reduction of inflation will bring a major bonus in the form of increased financial saving.

Although, as already mentioned, the policies followed by Chile have received support in international financial circles, some would argue that the reforms were not far reaching enough! The continuing segmentation of the financial market in leading to extremely high interest rates would be a major point in this argument. So would continuing, albeit smaller fiscal deficits (Sjaastad, 1984). Without a major revival of world economic activity, therefore, it appears that Chile will be called upon to pursue further the stringent policies it has already applied with such contentious results.

CONCLUSIONS

The implication of the current account financing patterns reviewed in Chapter 2 was that any international debt problems would increasingly have to be seen as dominated by the international indebtedness of the major Latin American republics. In seeking an answer as to why these countries had experienced difficulty, the chapter ended with a brief survey of aggregate investment and savings behaviour. Even at this level the pattern was mixed, with Brazil and Mexico giving some support to the 'investment shifts' argument in the form of relatively high ratios of investment to income. Other republics, however, did not display this characteristic. More generally there was evidence of rather poor domestic savings performance and, as the focus shifted to the two countries studied in the present chapter, this suspicion appeared to be justified.

Therefore, although both countries experienced a severe deterioration in external conditions, especially towards the close of our period, internal domestic policies have been relevant in the dynamics of debt accumulation. Similarly, although low real interest rates available in world capital markets for much of the period would encourage such borrowing, a substantial part of the attraction would be the contrast with extreme domestic financial market distortions, especially in the case of Chile. In some ways the countries facing the greatest problems with external debt prompt the observation that international debt difficulties are in part a reflection of the perverse responses of inflationary Latin American economies to fairly severe stabilization policies. In much the same way as lagged inflationary expectations have conduced to historically high world interest rates in recent times (thus adding to the problems of international debtors), the debtors themselves appear to have suffered from the collision between internal rigidities and a changing emphasis of financial policy.

NOTE

1   All growth rates were calculated on the basis of a fitted semi-log trend.

4 Financial intermediation, maturity transformation and inter-bank activity

In our introductory discussion of the relationships between 'real' and 'financial' crises two important aspects were suggested. Firstly, there was the relationship between the accumulation of debt in relation to the expected earnings of the borrower, supported by consideration of the structure of the debt. Secondly, there was mention of the potential importance of financial innovation in supporting changes in the pattern of indebtedness. In Minsky's cycle model, for instance, there is the argument that in the upswing financial innovation occurs to meet the burgeoning needs of optimistic borrowers. In particular innovations in short term lending are said to run ahead of other types conducing inadvertently to the ultimate difficulties of the borrower.

The first element has now been related in some detail to the context of international indebtedness. Growing debt relative to other sources of finance has been noted, as has the highly skewed distribution of the debt between countries. As to whether or not the level of borrowing has been 'excessive', much of what has been said is reassuring. While resource transfer to areas of capital scarcity is an underlying factor, it has arguably been supported in recent years by a *widening* of the gap between the marginal returns to investment in DCs and (some) LDCs. The major borrowing countries do seem to have sustained a high ratio of investment spending to GNP.

Moreover, the growth of this debt, measured in real terms, has been considerably less than the nominal values seemed to suggest and much borrowing could be explained simply as an attempt to prevent early repayment of capital in an inflationary environment. Indeed looking at the current situation, the point has been made that even the most heavily indebted countries (such as Argentina, Brazil and Mexico) have a public sector debt to GDP ratio of about one-third. This is the same as that of the government of the United States (Sjaastad, 1983, p. 315).

Nevertheless, it is the case that something of a generalized debt crisis did emerge in 1982–3. Most immediately the historically high levels of world interest rates made debt service considerably more onerous, as did, incidentally, the international value of the dollar. In addition, the recession in export markets clearly made the situation more difficult as a transfer problem. Although our two case studies have stressed the real importance of these influences, they have also shown the contribution of domestic policies which have had perverse results, particularly on the side of domestic savings performance. Both external and internal factors, then, contributed to the evident radical reappraisal which occurred in international banking circles in the early 1980s. At least temporarily the level of debt in some countries came to be regarded as 'excessive', and the contractionary programmes instituted, usually under IMF auspices, have been seen as critical in the maintenance of bank finance at prevailing levels. Recent arrangements will be referred to again in the next chapter.

Having suggested the main factors behind the emergence of this situation from the point of view of difficulties of the borrower we are left with the major issue to discuss. Why did the banks become so heavily involved that the present difficulties of a few, albeit major, borrowers should come to threaten the stability of the banks and the banking system?

The present chapter begins the analysis by looking at the nature of the emerging demand for intermediation and hence of the comparative advantage of banks in supplying it. It is shown that the key demand was for maturity transformation in which banks are traditionally specialized. However, the maturity transformation was effected in this case on the basis of wholesale (as opposed to retail) deposits, which has heightened the need for liability management and for a growing market in inter-bank loans. The inter-bank market is considered in this connection at the end of the chapter and as one possible source of system-wide banking risk in consequence of the close linkages between institutions obtaining there.

Such risks of system dislocation, however, rest on the risks of certain individual institutions: today on the country exposure of major banks. Hence Chapters 5 and 6 are addressed to the question of why this exposure reached the levels it did. Chapter 5 reviews many of the arguments previously advanced in this connection and places them in the context of certain analytical features of loan markets.

In Chapter 6 this analysis is supported and, hopefully, carried further by a case study of the behaviour of two major banks. What can be learned about the emergence of such institutions at the centre of fears over international banking? A major contention, consistent with the evidence presented, is that the nature of new competition in banking tended to endogenize the extent of risk perception, especially in the context of the time. According to this thesis there is good reason why bankers chose to take seriously the optimistic views attributed to them and reviewed in Chapter 5.

What, then, were the main features of international financial market developments in the 1970s? Early discussion of the development of the Eurocurrency market centred on the potential impact on global inflation of its rapid growth. The outcome, though not the detail, of this debate is relevant for present assessment in that it has led to a clearer view of what Eurocurrency assets and liabilities actually represent. In so doing some of the important risk issues in international borrowing by LDCs are thrown into relief:

A Eurocurrency is simply a foreign currency deposited in a bank outside the country where the currency is issued as legal tender. A dollar deposited in New York is a plain dollar, but it becomes a Eurodollar when deposited in a bank outside the United States. [Mendelsohn, 1980, p. 18.][1]

As these deposits, like conventional deposits, are on-lent, the size of the Eurocurrency market may be seen in terms of foreign currency liabilities or claims of banks. Gross and net measures of the size of the market differ by estimates of inter-bank depositing so that the net size of the market would be the measure of direct relevance to the non-bank sector. Two series are offered in Table 4.1 to indicate orders of magnitude. The first set are derived from BIS (Bank for International Settlements) data and the second from Morgan Guaranty, as both are frequently quoted.

Both sources in Table 4.1 suggest very similar (semi-log) trend rates of growth for gross *and* net claims of around 22–23 per cent per annum over the ten year period. Annual change in gross claims is slightly lower in the BIS statistics (20 per cent), but given the procedure outlined in note (b) to the table, the safest conclusion would be that gross and net positions have grown at similar rates, implying that inter-bank activity has developed alongside transactions with the non-bank sector.

This considerable growth during the 1970s following a similar performance (though from a much smaller base) in the 1960s led to renewed emphasis on potential implications for global economic stability. Literature appearing in the early 1970s concentrated on the creation of global liquidity through multiple deposit expansion in the Eurocurrency market. The main focus of this debate was over the size of the alleged 'initial deposit multiplier'. If, for instance, an American owner of a demand deposit in a domestic bank were to be attracted by high interest rates offered on Eurodollar deposits in a London bank, a book-keeping transfer could allow him to benefit. He would instruct his bank to debit his account with the necessary amount in favour of

Table 4.1 *International bank lending: bank loans outstanding*
($ billions)

	1972	1973	1974	1975	1976	1977	1978	1979	1980	1981
(1) Gross Eurocurrency lending	164	241.3	385.8	340.7	416.5	502	664.5	838.6	994.5	1,134.3
(2) Net lending	120.6	172.1	214.6	254.6	324.6	399.6	535	665	810	940
(3) Gross liabilities of Eurobanks	210	315	395	485	595	740	950	1,220	1,515	1,655
(4) Net lending	110	160	220	255	320	390	495	615	755	855

Notes: (a) Row 1 is derived from BIS annual data following the approach adopted by Hogan and Pierce (1982, p. 73). On the grounds that the bulk of foreign lending by Canadian and Japanese banks is in foreign currency these authors add to reporting European banks' foreign currency lending the international loans, reported by BIS, of banks in those two countries. To this total is added loans by branches of US banks in so called 'off-shore' centres, although part of this undoubtedly reflects US origin dollar deposits switched to these centres by American banks and destined for re-lending in the US. This procedure, at certain times, has avoided US imposed reserve requirements. (b) Row 2 is BIS net international lending and is somewhat overstated as a measure of Eurocurrency funding since international lending by European banks *in domestic currency* is included. Other than this, the difference between rows 1 and 2 reflects inter-bank activity. Row 2, however, does not exclude *all* inter-bank transactions, mainly (i) positions with banks *outside* the BIS reporting area, (ii) bank transactions with member central banks and the BIS itself, (iii) transactions by reporting banks in their *domestic* currency with banks in other reporting countries. Here, the first bank is regarded as a proximate 'borrower' or 'user' of Eurocurrency funds which the net market size must encompass. Detail on the BIS accounting is given in Mayer (1976). (c) Rows 3 and 4 take in a somewhat wider coverage including Bahrain and the Netherlands Antilles along with wider coverage of the Hong Kong and Singapore markets (Morgan Guaranty).

the London institution. The latter would then own the US demand deposit balanced by a liability in the form of a Eurodeposit owned by the American citizen.

   The initial effect of this transaction is to leave the American money supply, comprising demand deposits in US banks, unaffected since the ownership alone of the deposit has changed. A London bank, however, is now the owner of that 'cash' deposit and is free to deploy it for gain. If it is loaned to a non-bank firm and used to buy goods in the USA, the ownership of the deposit reverts there and the process ends. On the other hand, if the firm used the loan to buy UK goods a foreign exchange transaction would be involved with sterling being exchanged for dollars and the Bank of England, through that transaction, becoming the owner of the US demand deposit. The important feature of this case is that 'world' foreign exchange reserves rise by the amount of the Bank of England's new dollar asset. A further possibility would be for the proceeds of the loan made by the London bank to be redeposited in the Eurocurrency market, thus allowing the process to be repeated in a (deposit) multiplier fashion. Such a multiplier could also be enhanced if, when central banks became owners of US demand deposits, as instanced with the Bank of England above, they were to redeposit them in the Eurocurrency markets. Indeed much of the debate over the size of the initial deposit multiplier depended on assumptions about the extent of 'leakages' from the Eurocurrency system, as in the case of the purchase of American goods above, and of central bank redepositing. The smaller the former and the larger the latter, the larger would be the multiplier.

Doubts concerning this reasoning emerged in at least two connections. Firstly, the analogy with the domestic bank credit multiplier was false in that Eurocurrency banking is wholesale and not retail banking and few reserves are held against Eurodeposits. The importance of this is that Eurobanks are able to balance their portfolios on the assets and liabilities sides without the obligation, as imposed on domestic retail banks, to hold low yielding cash reserves. This suggests that a potential inflow of new 'cash' into these banks would not automatically be accepted and re-lent if interest rates earned on such lending were to be low. Indeed automatic re-lending presupposes an excess demand for credit at prevailing interest rates which while plausible in a regulated domestic context is not in an unregulated wholesale banking market (Tobin, 1963). This reasoning suggests that the initial deposit multiplier would be substantially attenuated by interest rate effects. The initial dollar inflow outlined above would tend to drive Eurocurrency interest rates down, producing a reverse flow in favour of, say, domestic US time deposits (Hewson and Sakakibara, 1974).

The second criticism of the multiplier analysis, however, is more basic and more relevant for present purposes. Among the first to stress the point was an economist at the BIS in explaining that institution's conception of the net size of the Eurocurrency market as shown, for instance, in Table 4.1 (Mayer, 1976). In terms of the example given above the issue turns on the distinction between *credit* and *money*. If for instance Eurodeposits are regarded as 'money', then it is easy to generate a multiple expansion of world 'money' on that definition. (US money supply does not fall but Eurodeposits rise, as in the above example.) Clearly, however, this cannot directly be an *inflationary* increase in the world money supply since *spendable* dollars have not increased; that is, the only way in which a Eurodollar deposit can be spent is by converting it into a demand deposit, since this is the only deposit against which a cheque can be drawn in payment for goods. In the example given, the purchase of American goods is permitted by the drawing of a cheque against the US demand deposit. Similarly, expenditure on UK goods is only permitted by Bank of England supply of domestic sterling in exchange for the ownership of that US deposit.

It is crucial to recognize therefore that *spendable* money (e.g. M_1 as against a 'global' M_3) is not directly increased by Eurocurrency transactions, so the conclusion has to be that this is, primarily, a market in financial intermediation and, hence, credit rather than monetary creation. In retrospect much of the accidental growth of the Eurocurrency markets during the 1960s can be seen best in this light. Thus, a key determinant of that growth had been the response of the US authorities to a worsening of the official settlements balance of payments in 1964 and 1965. In 1964 the interest equilization tax was tightened to discourage borrowing by foreign residents on the American capital market. In 1965 this was reinforced by the voluntary foreign credit restraint program and the Office of Foreign Direct Investment. These programmes resulted from the buoyant mood of US business corporations at the time with regard to opening overseas plants. The programmes sought to reduce the impact of this on the American balance of payments by, among other things, greater borrowing abroad to finance foreign direct investment. This pressure on the demand for credit side coincided with the limitations imposed on the ability of domestic American banks to compete at home for large interest-bearing time deposits through the so-called 'regulation Q' of the Federal Reserve Board. Accordingly American banks opened branches abroad, notably in London, and competed for such deposits there for purposes of on-lending to their corporate American customers and their foreign subsidiaries. As Mendelsohn argues:

> The combined effect of all this nonsense was therefore little else than to remove a large part of the American money and capital markets offshore where, having discovered many advantages (like lower taxes and freedom from officially imposed reserve requirements), much of the markets have remained [Mendelsohn, 1980, p. 34].

In this way, therefore, the markets were *substituting* for domestic financial intermediation; they were not directly adding to global inflation as available domestic credit was merely being transferred to corporate customers by way of London and other 'offshore' centres.

On this basis any global expansionary or inflationary impulse could only result directly from an increase in the *velocity of circulation* of the existing money supply and not from an expansion of the stock of money. There is, however, an important indirect route to such an outcome implicit in what has already been said about the tendency of the market to facilitate the expansion of world reserves. Triffin has recently pointed to this as evidence of the potential of present world monetary arrangements to cause global inflation (Triffin, 1982). In terms of our present interests, however, these two points (velocity and reserve increases) can best be developed in terms of the more recent 'recycling' context.

In the domestic financial system, the emergence of a new form of financial intermediation can be expansionary if it results in a saving in the use of the existing stock of money balances. If it is assumed that the latter, comprising cash plus bank demand deposits (on which cheques may be drawn), are controlled by monetary authorities, anything which reduces demand for these assets will permit expansion; that is, the initial demand reduction would require some mixture of an increase in incomes or prices and a reduction of interest rates as a means of re-establishing the equality between demand and the controlled supply of money balances. If, for instance, a new financial intermediary offers an attractive rate of return, or service, in exchange for cash deposits which deposit holders do not immediately wish to spend, ownership of the deposit will be transferred to the intermediary in exchange for its own liability.[2] In turn, the intermediary may re-lend the deposit to a borrower for immediate expenditure and in this way the velocity of circulation is increased. The banks themselves, if, for instance, deposits are constrained by the supply of cash, would be less easily able to perform this function. Only if depositors could be persuaded to switch from demand deposits to time deposits, and if the latter required a smaller cash : deposits ratio, would they be able to increase their lending. The additional expansionary feature of non-bank intermediation is that reserves held by the non-banks are themselves bank deposits and not controlled cash base. If supply of cash base is binding, further economy in its use is permitted (Grabbe, 1982).

This background can be used to indicate how the international banks (Eurobanks), acting as intermediaries, helped initially to prevent the full deflationary impact of the oil price shocks of the 1970s on the *world* economy from being realized. It was widely argued at the time that these increases acted as a tax on the major Western economies and were deflationary to the extent that the OPEC producers were unable to spend their new revenues. The conclusion drawn from this was that expansionary government spending policies were necessary to offset the deflationary gap. This was roughly equivalent to the argument that the world's average propensity to 'save' had increased and that the bulk of this saving would be in money or 'near' money (bank time deposits) balances. According to the previous argument the banks may have been unable, alone, to expand their lending to match the increase in desired saving, with classic Keynesian consequences as velocity of circulation declined.

Given the desire of the OPEC countries to maintain their funds in liquid ('near' money) form, the way in which Eurobank intermediation offset this outcome becomes more clear. By offering an attractive package (including anonymity and location outside the USA combined with reputable banking names), the Eurobanks secured many of the newly acquired OPEC deposits from domestic banks in the United States and elsewhere. These could then be on-lent, facilitated by a lack of legal *cash* reserve requirements together with prudential reserves generally comprising *deposits* held at their head offices.

This transfer to the Euromarkets alone, however, would not itself be sufficient to prevent a decline in velocity or, indeed, a *reduction* in the global money supply. Both could still occur, for instance, if the initial oil price rises led to a payments deficit (as in fact occurred in a less than freely floating exchange rate regime) and a resulting loss of oil-importing countries' foreign exchange reserves. If the financial effects of the deficit were not sterilized the reserve loss would imply a *reduction* of the domestic monetary base. Assuming that the governments of countries in this position borrowed the newly deposited Eurofunds to rebuild their reserves, the original reduction in domestic money would not be reversed. The net effect would be that the central bank of the country concerned would have in its books an *unchanged* total of foreign exchange reserves on the assets side. The liabilities side would be unaffected, with liabilities to the government now increased by the same amount as liabilities to domestic banks declined (Argy, 1981 pp. 91 and 96).

This type of behaviour was undoubtedly important, as Argy's analysis demonstrates, but if this was the end of the process it would be difficult to argue that world economic activity had been sustained by Euromarket intermediation. In terms of the earlier discussion of domestic intermediation what is implied so far is that OPEC savings had been passed on to borrowers *not* for direct expenditure but simply to hold as liquid assets against contingencies (oil-importing countries replenish foreign exchange reserves). Additionally, the intermediation now leads to a leakage of domestic money from the system.

For the major borrowing nations in the developing world, as we have seen, however, governments did maintain economic activity levels, on the basis of borrowing from international capital markets, to an extent which significantly sustained OECD economic activity. Financial intermediation from surplus (OPEC) countries to deficit *spending* LDC governments did indeed take place in addition to the reconstitution of reserves.

The use of Euromarket borrowing for these two distinct purposes, however, raises an essential point in the process of international financial intermediation. If governments merely wished to borrow to reconstitute their reserves following terms of trade shocks, the funds borrowed could be redeposited at similar maturities and 'rolled over' (renewed) as necessary at little cost. Conversely, if funds were only available for short-term borrowing (without confidence of renewal at the end of the stated term), any expenditure so financed would have to lead to adequate returns in time to repay the loan. Clearly, however, the volume of expenditure undertaken by LDCs on the basis of foreign borrowing could not have been expected to have such a profile of returns. In particular, projects financed through government foreign borrowing either directly, or with loans to the private sector, would have returns in tax revenues and loan service payments stretching over a number of years.

As we have already noted, however, the OPEC countries exhibited a marked preference for placing their funds on short term deposit and the implication must be that effective 'maturity transformation' took place.[3] On the face of it, though, significant maturity transformation is surprising in what is a *wholesale* international capital market. Whereas the conventional 'retail' banking sector is characterized by a large number of relatively small individual deposits, wholesale banks accept a small number of large deposits. In this context 'small' and 'large' deposits are relative to the institutions' total operations. Maturity transformation is a natural feature of retail banking as demand deposits (themselves accepted as money) are translated by the banks into loans or overdrafts of various maturities. The viability of this operation of course is the 'stochastic' principle whereby only a small proportion of the large number of depositors wish to withdraw cash at any one time, and this may be met by the holding of fractional cash reserve (Artis and Lewis, 1981, p. 101).

This principle of course cannot be utilized in the wholesale case where large individual deposits are held. In such markets deposits are time deposits with a predictable withdrawal pattern and, as such, loans made by the intermediary concerned must be compatible with the maturity pattern of the deposits. Accordingly, traditional theories of wholesale banking have emphasized economy of transactions costs as an explanation of the margin between borrowing and lending rates on which the intermediaries' profits rest (since both rates must be for similar 'maturities' and they cannot receive a return for the production of 'liquidity'). Some maturity transformation may take place if intermediaries believe that long term interest rates differ from the average of short term rates to be expected over the same period. If long term rates seem relatively high on these expectations the banks will accept shorter term deposits and lend for longer durations, relying on refinancing these claims at lower interest rates as each deposit is repaid. As Artis and Lewis point out, however, this reasoning would be expected to produce evidence of modest maturity transformation in *both* directions with institutions sometimes also borrowing 'long' to lend 'short' (Artis and Lewis, 1981, p. 97). The reasoning here would be the implausibility of the intermediaries holding *persistently* differing beliefs from the market as a whole. Given the limited period over which such predictions may reasonably be made this theory suggests that maturity transformation could be marginal as well as varying in direction.

In contrast to such expectation the evidence for the Eurocurrency market is of significant maturity transformation which is persistently positive, with intermediaries accepting funds of shorter maturity than the loans they make. One technique for displaying the extent of maturity mismatching of claims and liabilities is an adaptation of the Lorenz curve first used in this context by Hewson (1975, Ch. 3). The procedure here is to arrange assets and liabilities into uniform classes of maturity and to calculate the cumulative percentage up to and including each class as length of maturity increases. The two cumulative percentages can then be related graphically.

If, in each maturity class, liabilities and claims were matched precisely, the result would be the diagonal of the square depicted in Figure 4.1. In practice it is positive maturity transformation that is relevant, as indicated by the curve of increasing slope. As we start the calculations from the shortest maturity group (nearest the origin), this curve suggests that a higher proportion of liabilities than assets is accounted for here. As the maturities lengthen a more rapidly growing proportion of claims is accounted for with little increase in the percentage of liabilities. For comparison of a number of cases the same information can be presented in the form of a ratio which relates the area between the transformation curve and the diagonal (hatched in Fig. 4.1), to the area of the right-angled triangle above or below the diagonal. Thus, the larger the numerical value of the ratio (bound between −1 and +1) the greater the maturity transformation.[4]

Data which permits this calculation for the portion of the Eurocurrency market located in London (about 45 per cent of the total) is provided by the Bank of England for foreign currency claims and liabilities of banks located in the UK. These are broken down by ownership, and maturity patterns for those institutions can be calculated for liabilities and claims relative to a number of sectors. Table 4.2 presents the calculations for four years for each group with respect to (a) the London Eurocurrency inter-bank market, (b) banks overseas and (c) other overseas residents.

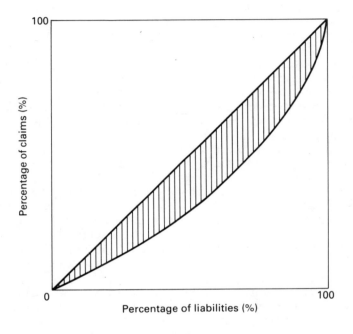

Figure 4.1

It is clear from the sectoral breakdown in Table 4.2 that the bulk of maturity transformation taking place in the London segment of the Eurocurrency market is in bank dealings with the non-bank sector. The case of direct interest shown is in transactions with the non-bank, non-resident sector. Apart from the significant degree of maturity transformation depicted, it is also noteworthy that the pattern for the various nationalities of banks seems to be rather stable for the years shown. This confirms the general impression (e.g. Grabbe, 1982, p. 66) that maturity transformation has changed by discrete 'jumps',

Table 4.2   *Maturity mismatch ratios for Eurocurrency claims and liabilities of banks located in the UK by ownership and sector*[a]

Re UK Inter-bank	1979	1980	1981	1982
Market				
British	–0.049	–0.09	–0.06	–0.024
American	0.169	0.15	0.21	0.301
Japanese	0.07	0.042	0.09	0.109
Other overseas banks	–0.053	–0.021	–0.035	–0.029
Consortium banks	–0.178	–0.106	–0.096	–0.065
Re banks abroad				
British	0.073	0.053	0.076	0.09
American	0.117	0.136	0.131	0.24
Japanese	0.074	0.053	0.052	0.114
Other overseas banks	0.117	0.072	0.112	0.139
Consortium banks	0.186	0.211	0.246	0.315
Re other non-residents				
British	0.644	0.702	0.65	0.724
American	0.599	0.586	0.547	0.574
Japanese	0.694	0.752	0.753	0.728
Other overseas banks	0.489	0.493	0.513	0.463
Consortium banks	0.758	0.764	0.808	0.808

Source: Bank of England Quarterly Bulletin (various issues), Appendix Tables 13 or 14.2.
[a] All data are as at November of the year indicated.

following the oil price increases, otherwise remaining stable. For example, the same ratio calculated for September 1973 taking all the banks together in their dealings with the non-bank sector was 0.358. As this in turn represented a pattern that had been stable for a number of years, Hewson concluded that 'on none of these dates did maturity transformation appear to be a significant characteristic of British Eurobanking operations' (Hewson, 1975, p. 67).

Evidently, maturity transformation of the magnitude depicted consistently in the years covered by Table 4.2 cannot be explained on the interest arbitrage principles mentioned previously. Moreover, the bulk of the loans concerned carry an interest rate explicitly tied to the short term LIBOR. The evidence of Table 4.2, however, now suggests a possible premium associated with liquidity transformation in a way somewhat analogous with the domestic retail banking system. In the present case, although the borrower now faces the risks of a rising LIBOR, the term of the loan is fixed and access to funds for the stated period is guaranteed. Similarly, the depositor retains access, in principle, to his deposit in reasonably 'liquid' (time deposit) form. The borrower, therefore, pays a premium for *illiquidity*. From the viewpoint of the lender, anecdotal evidence has to suffice, but banking circles confirm that, for example, Saudi Arabian authorities accepted a 'bulk discount' below short term rates on their very large deposits with major banks. They have been willing to accept this in exchange for *liquidity* whereas this would not have been the case for loans to ultimate borrowers. Indeed their contrasting lack of interest in direct lending to LDCs, through Eurobond issues, underlines the criticism made by Hogan and Pierce concerning international bank lending.

> Lenders can be induced to pass on funds to finance spending that they would not think of supporting if they knew the facts, and if, knowing the facts, they were required to carry the risk unsupported by an underwriting bank. [Hogan and Pierce, 1982, p. 86.]

Their concern in raising this issue is partly to emphasize the allocative inefficiency effects that may be engendered in loan markets,[5] but our own narrative suggests how the misallocation could take place. If ultimate savers had to be persuaded *to part with liquidity and to shoulder the associated loan risks themselves,* interest rates on international lending would probably be forced up. Accordingly, borrowers would have to reassess their position, perhaps undertaking more rapid balance of payments adjustment at some transitional real cost. In present circumstances the provision of intermediation, which 'produces' both liquidity and risk spreading reduces interest rates on loanable funds. The extent to which this precipitates over lending, however, depends on the soundness of judgement of the intermediaries, but their access to relatively cheap funds is certainly a force for expansion on the supply side. The pressures that may lead to actual overlending are more fully discussed in Chapters 5 and 6, however, and relate to the extent to which bankers exploited the comparative advantage revealed above.

Returning to the initial discussion of maturity mismatching in the context of a wholesale banking sector, the extent of maturity transformation indicated in Table 4.2 implies considerable reliance on 'liability management' to maintain the funding of a loan portfolio maturing later than the deposits which have financed it. Such institutions must enjoy market confidence to be able to do so and there must exist a market able to supply funds as and when required. Such a market, which brings together the major 'money centre' banks as suppliers of liquidity and other banks as demanders is the inter-bank market. It is of interest to refer to this specifically for two reasons. First, it has been argued that this market and its expansion have been essential for wholesale maturity transformation. Secondly, in forming an important link between the banks it provides one possible route for crises relating to one institution to be passed on to others. This has indeed already occurred.

In present circumstances we are concerned with the Eurocurrency inter-bank market, but the basic reasons for its existence are the same as those for the domestic (sterling) inter-bank market. The two in fact operate in parallel and arise out of a tendency for banks to be unequally specialized in deposit-taking and loan-making behaviour. If banks always had matching assets and liabilities there would be no purpose for the market. In fact such evenly balanced positions do not occur: some banks regularly receive more deposits than they have use for and others are short of funds for the loans they would like to make (Wills, 1982).

Estimates of the size of the total Eurocurrency inter-bank market are subject to considerable statistical uncertainty, but best guesses are that liabilities stood at between $900 and $1,335 billion at the end of 1980 (Ellis, 1981, Table B). A good deal of these large values may represent intra-bank balances (e.g. between subsidiaries and head office) and American information suggests that 50 per cent may be so accounted. Of banks located in the UK (as in Table 4.2.), the American banks are major net lenders to the market with the British and Japanese banks acting in the same direction though on a smaller scale. The Consortium banks are major net borrowers (presumably from their shareholder banks) (Ellis, 1981, Table A). This appears to be a consistent pattern. Similar consistency is found in the proportion of foreign currency liabilities of banks in the UK which are made up of inter-bank funds, as Table 4.3 suggests.

Our own ratios shown in Table 4.2 for the UK inter-bank market, and for transactions with overseas banks, suggest little maturity transformation within the banking sector. This conclusion is confirmed by Ellis's study of the global position. However, that author's conclusion that the evident maturity transformation that takes place in non-bank transactions must largely occur between that sector and the last bank in the inter-bank deposit chain need not be the only possibility.[6]

Alternatively, as Artis and Lewis suggest, the inter-bank market may provide a mechanism whereby wholesale maturity transformation can take place, allowing individual institutions *not* to be significantly mismatched in their own portfolios. They suggest two possible procedures:

(i)   Wholesale Bank A receives a large deposit. It seeks out some non bank customers, . . . [implying maturity transformation on these loans] . . . and lends the rest to Bank B via the interbank market. Bank B in turn loans out some to non-bank customers and the rest to Bank C etc. This method of sharing out the transformation can be done in this informal way *or formalised in the consortia principle and in syndicated loans* [italics added].

(ii)   Wholesale Bank C is approached for a loan by a non-bank customer on a 6 month roll-over basis and bids for 3 month interbank funds (liability management). Bank B supplies a 3 month interbank loan, itself accepting 1 month money from Bank A which has received a call deposit. [Artis and Lewis, 1981, p. 101].

Table 4.3   *Liabilities in foreign currencies of banks in the UK ($ billions; percentages in italics)*

End-period	All reporting institutions Total	Inter-bank	British banks Total	Inter-bank	American banks Total	Inter-bank	Japanese banks Total	Inter-bank	Other overseas banks Total	Inter-bank	Consortium banks Total	Inter-bank
1978, Q2	247.3	*60*	49.7	*57*	83.2	*49*	31.1	*65*	68.3	*68*	15.1	*81*
1979, Q1	292.2	*60*	57.9	*57*	90.1	*47*	44.4	*69*	81.8	*65*	17.8	*81*
1980, Q1	406.8	*59*	80.5	*57*	121.4	*44*	73.1	*74*	111.4	*65*	20.6	*80*
1981, Q1	513.9	*61*	108.1	*56*	128.5	*43*	116.6	*80*	133.8	*63*	26.7	*82*

Source: Ellis (1981), Appendix Table C.
Note: The inter-bank definition in this case differs from that of Table 4.2 in that intra-centre (i.e. UK inter-bank market) liabilities are added to liabilities to overseas banks and from this total is deducted liabilities to central banks (cf. Ellis, 1981, Appendix Tables A and B).

According to these important hypotheses, then, supply or demand side factors can precipitate wholesale maturity transformation by way of the inter-bank market, although inter-bank positions would remain, largely, balanced. Major banks, such as those discussed in Chapter 6, are in a position to act as net suppliers of deposits to this market and the number of participating banks funding their shares in syndicated loans through inter-bank channels grew rapidly over the period studied, emphasizing the importance of the procedures described.

If transformation has been effected this way we should examine the implications for system risk. The behaviour suggested in (i) above could be characterized by an 'inverted' bank credit multiplier where the 'leakage' in fact represents the percentage of each bank's deposit on which maturity transformation *is* carried out and the multiple deposit expansion is of inter-bank deposits. If for instance each bank undertakes maturity transformation for one-tenth of its deposit, placing nine-tenths with each bank in the chain, the familiar geometrical progression would suggest an eventual 'leakage' (into maturity-transformed loans) of the full amount of the initial deposit and inter-bank deposits of ten times this value![7]

This starkly simplified example, if reversed, serves to underline an important, and at first somewhat paradoxical point, that the inter-bank market, where maturities are closely matched, (cf. Table 4.2), and therefore most 'liquid', cannot be an ultimate source of *system* liquidity!

Thus, the capacity to liquify inter-bank funding depends upon the liquidity and debt-servicing capacity of the final non-bank borrower. [Hogan and Pierce, 1982, p. 90.]

The point here is somewhat analogous to the credit multiplier analysis of an open market sale of government securities in the domestic context. In this case, the initial deposit withdrawal represents a cash drain and although one bank may bid for deposits to replace those lost, the system as a whole cannot do so. Either (1) banks must reduce their lending and deposits in proportion to the loss of cash (i.e. reduce their balance sheets) or (2) the authorities must inject liquidity to prevent the credit contraction. The essential difference in the wholesale banking or maturity transformation case is that reducing the aggregate balance sheet would not be easy. It is, after all, for this reason that each bank keeps the bulk of its wholesale deposit finance in the form of closely matched inter-bank loans. Only the very largest wholesale participants could hope to have a sufficiently large portfolio of loans, conveniently maturing, adequately to balance the deposit drain. Seen in this light it may be argued that the maturity transformation witnessed above represents a potent risk since the inter- bank market makes the liquidity of the system appear greater than it would be if significant 'unwinding' of positions occurred.

Unwinding would be most likely to result if the major banks were to become concerned about the financial practices of certain participants. Given the strong linkages, and the sometimes questionable liquidity of inter-bank loans, there is a tendency for the entire market to be affected by the adverse experiences of one or a few participating institutions. Inter-bank rates are roughly paralleled by rates on Eurodollar certificates of deposit (CDs), and the tendency for the 'spread' between these rates and risk-free (Treasury Bill) rate to widen during banking scares has been clear (e.g. Anderson and Field,

1982). A specific early example of a severe deterioration in the market occurred in 1974 following the collapse of Bankhaus I. D. Herstatt. A more recent instance was the revelation that the Brazilian and Mexican authorities had instructed their banks to draw down inter-bank lines as a short term expedient to finance due sovereign loan service. The funds involved were therefore tied up in the debt rescheduling negotiations which followed, casting doubt on the liquidity of inter-bank funds in general. The number of institutions able to operate in the market was curtailed (Montagnon, 1983). A further, though somewhat removed, instance of the speed with which crisis can be reached in the market for inter-bank funds is provided by the UK secondary banking crisis of 1973–5 (Reid, 1982). The need there shown for a co-ordinated injection of funds to prevent a further spread of the crisis, to some of the biggest participants, is a highly relevant point in the present context.

Indeed, after this review of financial developments in the 1970s an important stage has been reached in the present study. The narrative has suggested that these financial developments reflected a burgeoning market for international credit. Those demanding the credit, in LDCs, evidently believed that international borrowing could be justified in terms of the investment and growth potential of their economies.

On the other hand, the newly rich savers in the OPEC countries were unwilling to buy 'primary' securities in the form of directly financing such investment, wishing instead to maintain a high degree of liquidity. The requirement of the financial system therefore was that it should shoulder the burden of risk and in fulfilling this requirement was able to provide finance to sovereign borrowers at highly competitive rates. This would be an influence depressing interest rates additional to the basic global savings–investment balance as emphasized by Sachs and referred to in Chapter 2.

Experience now shows that the banks exploited their opportunity and, in the process, had the socially beneficial effect of sustaining, in some measure, global economic activity. Since commentators in the 1980s have argued that the banks were imprudent in their response (e.g. Lomax, 1983), and since we now have the experience of the rescheduling crises of 1982, we now turn to bank behaviour prior to these events.

NOTES

1 This source contains an excellent brief review of the early origins and reasons for development, of the Euromarkets especially: see pp. 9–36.
2 For example, a building society or savings and loan account.

3   In this instance financial institutions would be 'borrowing short' to 'lend long'. Grabbe (1982) provides a comprehensive discussion of the means whereby total spending may rise through Eurocurrency intermediation including maturity transformation.
4   The ratio is calculated by Hewson (1975) as follows:

$$\text{Mismatch ratio} = \frac{0.5 \sum_{i=1}^{n} (L_{i-1} C_i - C_{i-1} L_i)}{5,000} .$$

L_i and C_i represent the *cumulative* percentages in maturity class i and 5,000 is the area of the percentage triangle.
5   A Keynesian, rather than neoclassical, standpoint would perhaps suggest that waste of resources through global recession may be more pertinent as an argument in favour of recycling, even if some allocative inefficiency occurs.
6   Discussion with banks, however, indicates that they are frequently of this opinion regarding their own dealings in the market.
7   Objections to the mechanistic multiplier are clearly valid here. However, there are many reasons why banks may be specialized in their lending and borrowing behaviour and such a chain therefore becomes a plausible approximation.

5 Credit markets, loss risk, and the forces of expansion

We have now reviewed the major developments in the world economy during the 1970s together with the quantity and nature of the massive increase in financial intermediation with which these real changes were associated. With maturity transformation at the heart of the financial process we turn in this and the next chapter to the risks being incurred by the intermediaries effecting the transformation.

Following a brief review of the risks particular to country lending, the present chapter will set the optimistic arguments, deployed by bankers in the 1970s, in the context of the critical role played in credit market equilibrium by the assessment of default risk. Credit rationing is explained in this context together with its direct links, when default risks are reassessed, to the need for debt rescheduling as it emerged in the early 1980s.

The subsequent chapter examines the expansion into overseas lending from a different angle – that of the experience of two individual banks. Since the risks of a banking institution, as distinct from a subset of its loans, depend upon the composition of the overall balance sheet, the focus of the analysis will be on balance sheet developments. What can be learned from these developments and, in particular, what sort of adjustments were being made by the banks as the decade of the 1970s progressed? How did they respond to growing competition in overseas loan markets? It will be suggested that the competitive environment significantly influenced the manner in which country risks were assessed.

To begin, therefore, what are the risks facing banks in making sovereign loans? It will be convenient to relate these to other more general risks arising from intermediation which may be termed the interest rate, credit and liquidity risks (Goodman, 1981). The interest rate risk arises from the basic procedure of borrowing short and lending long. If the liabilities (deposits) are of shorter duration than the corresponding assets (loans), the institution may find itself having to 'fund' the loan (seek alternative finance) at higher interest rates than the yield on the assets. If interest rates are volatile, this risk can be important and lies behind the dominance of variable loan rates in LDC lending to be discussed.

Credit risk is fundamental and relates to the inability of the borrower to repay the debt while liquidity risk arises when a normally solvent intermediary suffers from an unexpected withdrawal of deposits. If assets cannot readily be liquidated, the institution would face an emergency and it is against this risk that liquid assets are held, in some prudential proportion, in the domestic banking context.

International lending of any kind poses an additional risk for the institution, to the extent that 'open' positions in foreign exchange are involved. Thus, any lending in excess of borrowing in a particular currency implies risk if exchange rates fluctuate. For the longer time periods involved in sovereign lending this risk is not readily covered in forward foreign exchange dealings. In addition to possibly enhanced foreign exchange risks, the liquidity risk may also be increased, as might another specialized form of risk somewhat related to credit risk as already defined. This particular form is commonly referred to as 'country risk'.

As to liquidity risk, the problem is one of the large size of individual wholesale deposits involved in Eurobanking. As far as the *individual receiving bank* is concerned, such a deposit presents two problems. First, there is the question of 'placing' the funds at short notice, which would mean finding one or two large borrowers, or passing the problem on by placing the funds in the inter-bank market. Chapter 6 will suggest that this has not been a major problem in practice. Secondly, however, once the funds have been utilized, there is the risk of sudden withdrawal.[1]

If we now turn to the topic of credit risk and place it in the context of international lending, we come to the main concern of the present chapter, the risk perceptions of banks regarding loans to foreign countries, assuming the other risks discussed are deemed acceptable. In this context the credit risk is largely superceded by *country* risk. Whereas credit risk referred to the inability of a borrower to repay his loan, or to meet the terms of its servicing, country risk may supervene even if the borrower *is*, in principle, able to do so. Thus, a loan to an individual, or enterprise, in a foreign country may fall foul of a *transfer* problem, even if the enterprise remains viable, simply because of the non-availability of foreign exchange with which to effect loan payment.

To the extent that the majority of bank lending to developing countries is public, or publicly guaranteed (by government or government agencies), the transfer problem may be ameliorated by the ability of the borrowing country to make debt repayment a priority use of foreign exchange. If, however, foreign exchange cannot be made available to service loans, we have something similar to credit risk at the national rather than the enterprise level. The difference is that whereas credit risk relates to possible *insolvency,* country risk arises with potential international (foreign exchange) *illiquidity.* Such an outcome could be the result of defective economic policy resulting in national over-absorption and/or unforeseen external developments rendering debt service impossible to maintain on the original terms. A substantial shortfall of export earnings would be an example of the latter circumstance as, indeed, would be a sudden rise in the price of an essential import. It is unlikely, however, that a nation would not have assets *ultimately* to repay the debt.

> Mexico owes $85 billion. Is Mexico worth $85? Of course it is. It has oil exports of $15 to $20 billion. It has gold, silver, copper. Has all that disappeared over the past week? [Anderson and Field, 1982, p. 19.]

This comment by a leading banker at the height of the 1982 Mexican rescheduling crisis epitomizes the distinction between illiquidity and insolvency and hence the basis for the soundness of sovereign lending as seen by the banking community.

Nevertheless international liquidity is only one of two components typically included in the notion of country risk. The second is the existence of sovereign immunity. When a loan takes place in the context of the domestic economy and a failure to maintain repayment terms occurs (default), bankruptcy proceedings may follow with tangible assets being liquidated to offset some of the loan loss. This is not the case with international loans to a government or government agency (Eaton and Gersovitz, 1980). Apart from the impracticability of seizure in this case, the legal context is difficult.

The notion of sovereign immunity in international law means that sovereign governments cannot be sued without their consent, that courts in one country will not usually pronounce on another country's behaviour within its own borders, and that the property of a government or its 'instrumentality' is immune, thus rendering any judgements actually made against it unenforceable (Angelini *et al.,* 1979, p. 77, which provides a fuller discussion). While lenders have sometimes negotiated waivers to these principles, it is clear that the security for loans in the international context is more precarious than for the domestic case.

An important implication for the lender to recognize is that a sovereign government may *choose* to default on (or repudiate) its debts if the discounted present value of the repayment flows were to exceed the anticipated benefits of continuing current loan service payments; that is, the lender may be faced with total loss of both interest and principal on the sovereign loan concerned. The prospect of total or partial non-repayment is a distinguishing feature of loan markets and can, on theoretical grounds, lead to 'credit rationing' in which the market is characterized by equilibrium off the demand schedule.

The essential feature of this literature is that some form of default probability function is required to arrive at a 'rationed' equilibrium. At the centre of the analysis is the role of imperfect information and uncertainty regarding borrower intentions (Akerlof, 1970; Jaffee and Russell, 1976). The Jaffee and Russell approach recognizes the central problem that there are dishonest borrowers (or merely 'unlucky' ones), who will sometimes default on loan repayment intentionally, or by force of circumstance. The dishonest borrower in this model is concerned only with two periods and will default whenever the penalty for doing so is less than his repayment obligations. An additional essential feature is the assumption that the *proportion of individuals* who default (after a minimal level of loan) is a rising function of loan size: people are more likely to be induced to behave dishonestly assuming that the penalties for default are distributed continuously throughout the population of borrowers. There is therefore no hard and fast distinction between honest and dishonest borrowers and creditors cannot distinguish them *ex ante*. There are, however, 'pathologically honest' borrowers (who fully intend to repay all loan obligations), for whom a demand function for loans can be specified and which will be *copied* by potentially dishonest borrowers in order to avoid detection.

In this context of anonymity before the event, the mechanism which brings about credit rationing is as follows. As the average size of loans increases, the number of defaults increases. If, therefore, loan size is restricted, defaults decline and the savings so achieved are passed on in a competitive loan market to borrowers. The honest borrower, therefore, is willing to accept credit rationing (obtaining smaller loans than he would like to have at the prevailing interest rate), in exchange for a lower rate of interest charged on the loan.

While this approach cannot apply directly to differentiated (country) borrowers, and the setting of country limits, an important variant has been developed to provide a rationale for country limits and which assumes that all borrowers are potentially dishonest (Eaton and Gersovitz, 1981). This assumption that borrowers will default if it suits them is a recognition of the special nature of sovereign lending already discussed, viz. that default can occur without loss of assets.

Despite this universal dishonesty, a stable loan market can still be established because borrowers are now optimizing, not only over two periods but over the indefinite future. The major penalty for default in this model is lack of access to loan markets (for ever after) and therefore of the possibility of 'smoothing' future income streams (the benefit of borrowing). In these conditions, a decision by the borrower *not* to default this year gives him access to further borrowing next year and a chance to reconsider whether default may be optimal.

In these circumstances, he is only in a positon to 'demand' credit if he does *not* default on loan obligations this year (each loan is repaid the following year). His decision on how much to attempt to borrow is based on an effort to maximize the utility gained from present and future consumption. Maximization of the latter may or may not involve default at a later time but, importantly, very heavy borrowing now in the half expectation of default next period is discouraged (a) by the fact that default *then* will preclude future access and (b) heavy repayment obligations next year, even if made, will reduce his access to credit then, since lenders see the probability of default as, in part, a function of repayment obligations. In this framework, the borrower is likely to borrow more if interest rates fall, other things equal, since this increases his potential consumption and credit limits if he should decide next year to postpone default to another period. It also directly discourages such a default decision by making loan repayments cheaper. On similar long term optimization grounds, even a potentially dishonest borrower could well prefer a credit-rationed solution along the lines presented above for honest borrowers.

'Country limits' follow naturally from this model since, unlike in the previous one, borrowers are distinguishable *ex ante* on certain characteristics which would help to indicate the point at which they would be likely to default. Country limits are applied in competitive equilibrium to try to prevent such points being reached and thereby to reduce the interest rate on loans actually made. Accordingly, countries for which the penalties of default would be high, for instance those with highly variable income streams, would be granted higher credit limits. On this reasoning, country risk assessment would lead directly to the establishment of country limits by the lender.

The importance of these theories for present purposes is their emphasis on the inadequacy of the price mechanism alone to determine the allocation of credit. Emphasis instead is on the assessment by lenders of the *probability* of full, or partial, failure to repay loans on the agreed terms. Such assessment, however, is inherently difficult and especially so given the rapidly changing circumstances of the 1970s and 1980s. The credit-rationing models assume that lenders 'know' the default probability function. This, in turn, would imply considerable pertinent experience which arguably did not apply in the 1970s and, given external changes, probably does not apply in the 1980s. Highly subjective calculations must be involved and may well account for the tendency for difficulties in one debtor country to be reflected in the market conditions facing other borrowers. The tightening of conditions facing most Latin American debtors in the aftermath of the Falkland Islands hostilities is a case in point.

Even if default probabilities were known, there remains the problem of how a stable, credit-rationed equilibrium is to be arrived at. In the early Jaffee and Russell model an individual borrower and a single contract is considered in which the progress towards rationed equilibrium is easily demonstrated. Although the Eaton–Gersovitz formulation assumes a similar mechanism it is not clear how it would operate in practice when the borrower can approach more than one lender over time. Even if each lender has full information on total borrowing to date, *future* borrowing plans by the country are not known. Moreover, the means open to the lender to influence the borrower's later behaviour, e.g. by varying the terms of future loans, remain weak for precisely the reason that the price mechanism is weak in the first place (Bond and Briault, 1983).

Given, then, a central role analytically for lender uncertainty, it is interesting to note the initially highly optimistic view taken of sovereign lending by bankers and which might still be supported in view of the absence to date of debt repudiation by such borrowers.

The general point made when contrasting sovereign with domestic lending was that whereas bankruptcy laws provide some creditor protection in the domestic context they are, at least in the context of a limited liability enterprise, confined to the liquidation value of assets. Beyond this point, the firm, and hence the security, is eliminated. With sovereign lending to national governments, however, the country involved is highly unlikely to disappear as an entity. Although legal remedies are limited, for reasons explained above, the penalties for default (failure to maintain the terms of loan servicing), and especially for repudiation (a government disowning an existing loan), are none the less severe.

Borrowing countries depend, more or less heavily, on trading links with creditor nations. Primary producing countries experiencing volatile export proceeds may want to borrow in future periods to smooth the domestic adjustments that would otherwise be required as commodity prices declined. Exclusion from short term trade finance, medium term borrowing and the ability to supplement domestic with foreign saving against longer term development prospects would be a great loss. Although not usually articulated, such sanctions would be particularly damaging for the political elites of the borrowing countries, whose own interests are inextricably linked with continued financial and commercial access to the major creditor nations. Indeed, the potential consequences of financial estrangement are so severe that President Castro of Cuba is reputed to have advised the then Jamaican Prime Minister (Manley), after Jamaica had broken off negotiations with the IMF in early 1980, to avoid default at all costs (Economist, 1982).

The more concrete developments that would support this view lie in the institutional arrangements of the syndicated medium term Eurocurrency market which dominates medium and long term private lending to LDCs. While its initial development was a consequence of need to arrange very large loans, which an individual institution would have found difficult or impossible to provide, other features of its organization may be mentioned in the present context. First, the process of syndicating an individual loan across a number of participating banks reduces individual bank exposure to loss in the event of default. Additionally, however, by tying banks together, the penalty to the borrower of default is magnified. As the banks are typically based in more than one country, any unwillingness to repay could effectively preclude the borrower from further market access across the board. The original lenders would be unwilling to continue funding and other syndicates would be unlikely to step in. More than one creditor nation would no doubt be applying political pressure as a further consequence of syndication (Goodman, 1980).

For whatever reason, as soon as default was called, the fortunes of each creditor would depend on the success achieved in legal action to recover funds (where this is legally possible in terms of the loan agreement and where seizable assets exist). Most creditors would receive nothing and unless agreement could be reached that particular loan would have to be written off. If, on the other hand, default were not called, there would be some chance that negotiation, with all lending interests standing together, would lead to resumption of, albeit rescheduled, payments. To resolve this prisoner's dilemma situation, banks in the syndicated market inserted 'cross default' clauses into loan agreements. Accordingly, should default be declared on one loan, all other loans to that borrower would be declared in default also and these too would become due and payable. Given almost certain loss in such circumstances, this device assists self-discipline among the lenders, but it also protects them against selective default and, by implication, threatens the borrower with the full potential consequences of failure to repay.

In addition to such reasoning there was the argument (unstated by bankers), that international institutions and governments of industrial countries would be expected to come to the assistance of borrower states in major financial difficulty. The banks could in these circumstances 'externalize' their risks at the potential expense of the taxpayers in major economies (Cline and Weintraub, 1981).

Over and above the balance of the above arguments suggesting the comparative safety of sovereign lending, a number of bank-specific factors seem to have added further to the weight of opinion in favour of this view.

Thus, it has typically been the case that country risk assessments, of whatever form, have only been one of two major ingredients in bank lending decisions, and the determination of country limits. The usual practice is for country assessment, with differing emphasis on formal risk analysis, to be conducted by an economist, or economics department, within the bank. The assessment reports are provided for a 'controller of lending' and his credit committee, who would have current details on 'exposure' of the bank, together with information on total indebtedness for individual countries. A second input to this group is formed by a stream of loan proposals from lending officers 'in the field', who also provide current situation reports on conditions in the territories for which they are responsible. This co-ordination of the lending process has clearly been an attempt by bankers to make loan decisions on an adjudication basis between the two types of input. The adjudication aspect arises in that economics department reports are inclined on the cautionary side, whereas the loan proposals tend to an optimistic appraisal both of the individual loans and of the medium term prospects for the borrower countries. It has been suggested to the author, in conversation, that this optimism is partly attributable to the rather high degree of career mobility within the banks and, in particular, in their international assignments. The immediate career prospects for a lending officer are likely to be enhanced by the amount of business he is able to win in his area of activity. If, at a later date, difficulties are experienced with some of the loans involved, the individual concerned may well have moved on. Perhaps even more significant is that this high degree of career mobility is repeated in the credit committees themselves. Whether prudential considerations automatically dominate in such circumstance is open to doubt. Other factors promoting 'over-lending' suggested by bankers have been time lags in information gathering and use concerning current conditions in borrower countries. Thus, credit committees have taken decisions with very imperfect knowledge. The most obvious example here is the genuine surprise of the banking community at the level of short term borrowing by certain Latin American debtors in 1982. The surprise in this case is itself surprising since BIS data for short-term borrowing was available.

A further expansionary factor was that loans do *not* represent a single item to be assessed for risk and return. The potential expected returns to each new loan have tended to be higher than details of the individual loan suggest. For example, in one instance mentioned to the author, the Taiwan authorities insisted on a minimum quantity of funding in exchange for permission to open branches in Taipei. The profitability associated with the latter was high and the business that could be booked through the branch would not necessarily increase sovereign risk; i.e. a lot of profitable trade finance would be involved.

It is not only prospective new business that could be at risk, but existing relationships:

> The fundamental reasons for participating . . . [in a syndicated loan] . . . may well be less tangible . . . [than fees, spreads, etc.] . . . A bank that has a long-standing relationship with a particular client would find it hard to refuse a participation in a credit. A refusal, or a few consecutive refusals, could lose the account. [Saade, 1981.]

Such accounts may well comprise substantial arrangements for lucrative short term financing of international trade for the country concerned. In some cases, important existing assets in the form of branch offices within the borrowing country may be seen to be at risk if a deterioration in relations with the borrower government, following a loan refusal, were to take place. Whatever the disadvantages to a country of defaulting on international loans, bank nationalization has been widespread and relatively free of international sanctions.

These sources of borrower leverage are a useful reminder that borrowing countries are able to exert a degree of influence over the banks that smaller domestic clients cannot. The loan terms therefore would not represent the only, or even the most important, returns to be set against the risks of participation in individual loans. The strength of the borrower in this connection could well be economic size related, as this would determine in part the general opportunities available to the banks in business relations with that economy. Bankers also stress the role of political pressure from home governments to make certain loans. American bank loans to Latin America and German bank loans to the Eastern bloc are mentioned in this context.

In addition to the pressures to lend that we have discussed, at the height of the recycling of OPEC surpluses (following 1974 and 1979), the banks were also under extreme pressure on the other side of their balance sheets. As noted previously, this concerned the generation of substantial individual deposits. Banks traditionally favoured by the major oil-producing nations (often American 'money centre' banks) were certainly reluctant to turn away the very substantial funds offered, for fear of losing the account of the depositor. When this depositor could be Kuwait, the magnitude of the difficulty is apparent. The pressure to place such large, discrete amounts complemented the more ebullient and expansionary forces in the lending departments of the banks. Given the pressure from borrowers, it would not be surprising if, in such an atmosphere, the careful application of country limits, based on detached assessment of risk and return, gave way to some expediency in a competitive environment. It may be objected that a large supply of deposits need not force individual banks to lend to sovereign borrowers, given the existence of an inter-bank market where excess funds can be readily placed, or indeed of large supply of developed country government securities. Against this, a further factor for the American banks has been the importance attached to the return on total assets (ROTA) by bank analysts in the US. One study suggests that this has been the main factor behind the relatively small amount of net lending by US banks to the London inter-bank market. As the margins (between the bid and offered rates, LIBBR and LIBOR respectively) are small, such lending would provide a relatively small return on the funds employed relative to the terms on sovereign lending (Ellis, 1981).

It is still an open question whether the optimistic views over country risk, as summarized above, will be falsified by events despite present difficulties. One study of all the cases between 1956 and 1980 in which country borrowers had been unable to maintain loan terms, and had therefore required to reschedule, concluded that losses to lenders had been minimal. This judgement was based on a comparison of original and adjusted loan terms, each calculated on a present value basis (Hardy, 1982). Moreover all such losses had been borne by *official* creditors and not by private banks.

However, whereas past experience might lead to the conclusion that country default (in which the lender suffered loss as opposed only to the requirement to reschedule) was a negligible risk, the growing incidence of rescheduling itself implies that banks were increasingly seeking to limit their exposure. Table 5.1 depicts the pattern of rescheduling experience over the decade up to the emerging crisis of 1982.

Given the 1974 oil price increases, the escalation of rescheduling after 1980 reflects in part the bunching of maturities on loans taken out at that time (with typical repayment terms over eight years). External economic difficulties of debtors, as discussed in the examples of Chapter 3, were also involved. In fact the inability of countries to obtain new financing in international capital markets would be the proximate *explanation* for the rescheduling; that is, credit rationing,

Table 5.1   *Rescheduling of official and bank debt: annual payments due on affected debt and number of countries involved ($ millions)*

	1970	1971	1972	1973	1974	1975	1976	1977	1978	1979	1980	1981	1982 (estimate)
Countries	2	1	3	2	4	2	2	3	3	4	6	14	20
Amount	2,108	100	496	447	1,494	478	480	382	2,312	4,920	4,459	10,786	27,913

Source: *Euromoney*, August 1982, p. 21

however achieved, was increasing the demand for rescheduling, since, if new funds had been available, maturing debt could have been painlessly rolled over on the original terms of repayment (Cline, 1984, p. 208).

In terms, then, of the earlier discussion it could be said that the banks were evidently reassessing their views of default probability, however late in the day. The apparent suddenness of the change in view must in part be put down to the severity of the global recession and the implications for major debtors of the interest rate escalation which occurred. There is, however, an interesting parallel in the experience of the banks in trying to assess default probability; that is of country risk assessment. In both the United States and Europe the economics departments of banks had been developing country risk or 'early warning' models over much of the period (Angelini *et al.,* 1979; Anderson, 1982). Certainly, the large banks had devoted considerable resources to such efforts. Techniques ranged from formal 'early warning' models, intended to alert bank management to emerging debt difficulties of country borrowers, to qualitative, and more or less uniform, country reports intended to highlight significant trends and prospects.[2] Generally, American banks were in favour of the former quantitative approach whereas the UK banks tended to employ the latter. One influential example of the quantitative technique has been the 'logit' model. The aim here was to use statistical techniques to establish relationships between a country's economic and financial condition and the probability that it would experience debt servicing difficulty. These relationships were derived on the basis of *past* instances of debt rescheduling and non-rescheduling.

An example of the qualitative approach is provided by one large British bank in which the credit committee receives regular country reports from the economics department giving the latest available estimates of GDP and its decomposition. Short term predictions of GDP growth and prices are attempted (for the subsequent twelve months) based on recent budgetary information. Very brief comments follow on the prospects for key economic sectors such as agriculture, energy and industry with an attempt at more precision on the balance of payments out-turn. Developments in international reserve positions also receive attention. The political situation is briefly reviewed for the last twelve months and short to medium term prospects are considered. The reports end with general comments on the outlook for the coming year. Graphs of economic magnitudes and ratios over a five year period, incorporating the export–import gap, official reserves and the debt service ratio, together with the ratios of reserves to imports (with the all country average) are presented. Although these reports are structured similarly for each country, cross country comparison must be a matter of judgement, failing any numerical standard of comparison. This judgement is exercised by the credit committee in setting the country limits.

Thus, the qualitative approach rests finally on 'judgement' and will be no more or less satisfactory than the collective opinions of the credit committee. On the other hand a fundamental criticism of 'logit' and other quantitative models is that they gain apparent numerical precision only by reliance on past observation. The past, however, may no longer be a good predictor of the future and the forecasting ability of the models may therefore not extend beyond the time period of the data from which they were constructed. This criticism gained particular strength in the wake of the Iranian default and the Polish and Mexican reschedulings. The singular political difficulties associated with the first two and the vagaries of oil price movements so critical to the third were not predicted from the models employed. Similarly, models estimated on the basis of data for the early 1970s tended to *over* predict the incidence of debt rescheduling in the late 1970s. Cline (1984, p. 206) argues that this was in large part due to the change in underlying circumstances. In particular the models had failed to account for the easing of access to international credit markets for country borrowers. Paradoxically, then, while some banks were probably receiving signals of debt servicing difficulty, based on past experience, the expansion of bank lending itself was sufficient to at least delay the outcome predicted.

In such an uncertain atmosphere it is not surprising that the upheavals of the early 1980s led to a demotion of assessment techniques based on the medium term and an elevation of short term indicators of debt servicing difficulty. The focus shifted to short term financial developments which usually identify the rescheduling cases in immediate prospect. Thus, rescheduling occurs, proximately, as a result of a sharp deterioration in (foreign exchange) cash flow (Amex, 1984). Cash flow problems, however, need not be closely related to the economic viability of a country and its policies, *if the lenders are increasingly disinclined to make judgements about the latter.* Thus, cash flow difficulties may result from the bunching of amortization payments from a sudden rise in global interest rates or from an excessive concentration of short term debt, and can be avoided only if lenders are willing to lend on the basis of sound medium term prospects. A loss of self-confidence by the banks in making such judgements throws the focus of assessment on to short term difficulties. In the words of an executive of a British bank:

> Unless a country builds up its reserves in line with its debt and with its current account deficit, its liquidity ratios may decline sharply, which may be further influenced by the short-long balance of its external debt. It then becomes vulnerable to adverse market psychology, and if some banks decide to reduce their short term lines, a genuine cash crisis may be precipitated.

With this increased attention to short term cash flow considerations, a final trend in country risk assessment is noteworthy. This was the growing attention being given to the loan terms *actually achieved* in capital markets by sovereign borrowers as indicators of country risk (Carvounis, 1982, p. 18). Indeed, country risk tables are published on this basis providing an *ex post* indication of market assessment as suggested by the weighted spread.[3] The implicit assumption behind this procedure is that the markets covered are 'information efficient' in the sense that all pertinent information is already incorporated into the prices quoted (in this case the spreads). While there is no reason to doubt that this probably is the case for syndicated loan markets, the narrative above has suggested that the information so incorporated by lenders became increasingly dominated by shorter term considerations. Disappointment with the attempts to predict country risk over a longer period was responsible for this alteration of focus. On the efficient markets hypothesis, the interpretation of this would be either that longer term prospects had proved impossible to assess accurately (i.e. the information did not exist to be incorporated into the market price), or that the cost of acquiring the information was too high relative to the market opportunities afforded by its possession. Arguments of this type help to provide a case for continuing IMF involvement in country lending as discussed in the final chapter, and that such involvement has certainly been precipitated in the recent past will be noted shortly.

In summary the rescheduling explosion of 1982 had two major component causes. Primarily the deterioration of external trading and financial conditions coincided with, in some cases, defective domestic policies to produce a surge in the requirements for external financing at levels of activity then prevailing. To this may be added the bunching of refinancing requirements arising from debt incurred previously. Secondly, however, we must note a separate crisis in financial markets where default probabilities were being rapidly revised upwards leading, as our theoretical discussion indicated, to increasing severity of credit rationing. This credit rationing was the proximate cause of the need for rescheduling, and indeed of the domestic retrenchment by the borrowers. The financial market crisis, in turn, can be related to a movement away from consideration of more distant prospects by lenders to those of the immediate future. With such an orientation there emerges a self-fulfilling quality to the crisis since the variables considered increasingly reflected the difficulties caused by the tightening of financial markets. If, for instance, a country becomes unable to turn over its debts by access to further long term loans, it may be obliged to use short term credits. Since these will cause a deterioration in cash flow, the availability of credit will be further curtailed with lenders concentrating on short term indicators. The Amex report makes this clear (Amex, 1984).

As with the Minsky debt–deflation cycle then, the debt crisis of 1982 had financial as well as real economic causes and much of what has been said above suggests that the financial intermediation which evolved in the 1970s to fulfil the recycling role contained substantial elements of instability as real circumstances fluctuated.

Where, however, does this leave the riskiness of the banking system which is our main concern? How far has the early optimism of the banks, which fuelled the growing proportion of sovereign debt in their balance sheets, been contradicted in the experience of the 1980s?

In answering these questions we will begin with a brief outline of two major reschedulings taking place in recent times and their potential impact on bank earnings and risk. Since bank risk, however, must be seen in terms of the totality of the balance sheet, the following chapter complements the analysis above by examining the evolution of the balance sheets of two major American banks during the 1970s up to the crisis in 1982. The question to be addressed at this level will be how far the banks began to respond to changing perceived risk and, indeed, how far they were able to do so in the competitive environment of the time.

It is possible to date the 1982 debt crisis to 20 August 1982 when Mexico unilaterally suspended payment to ninety days on its external debt standing at around $80 billion. The immediate causes had been the strains induced by the falling level of oil prices and climbing world interest rates. Rising domestic inflation, stimulated in the short term by the attempt to reduce budget deficits arising from price subsidies on petrol, bread and other basic items, caused a capital outflow from the country's private sector. At least $9 billion left the country in this way during the preceding months of 1982. The suspension of foreign debt payment was part of the government's response to sharply declining foreign exchange reserves.

In response, the international community extended emergency financing. The United States prepaid for oil deliveries for her strategic reserve, and provided agricultural finance and a short term bridging loan from the Federal Reserve. Each device contributed equally to a total of $3 billion. European central banks supplied a similar bridging loan of $0.925 billion by way of the BIS. Export credits were also forthcoming for $2 billion. Perhaps even more significantly the IMF entered the picture by providing $3.7 billion over three years through the extended Fund facility and $200 million from Mexico's first credit tranche. The total value of the funds made available in this way was $14.7 billion. The importance of this was that *the Fund made this support conditional on an agreement of debt rescheduling with the banks and some increase in bank loans.*

Accordingly private banks provided $5 billion of new loans and entered into rescheduling negotiations for $19.5 billion worth of public debt and for $15 billion of private debt. These principal sums were originally due for payment between 1982 and 1984.

On the other side of the agreement the IMF negotiated a major move to fiscal contraction with the Mexican authorities. The budget deficit was scheduled to decline from 17.6 per cent of GDP in 1982, to 8.5 per cent in 1983, 5.5 per cent in 1984 and 3.5 per cent in 1985. The government also moved to a flexible exchange rate regime and effective wage controls. From the point of view of the international financial community the Mexican adjustment programme was dramatically effective. The fiscal targets were met, imports fell by 40 and 46 per cent in 1982 and 1983 respectively and non-oil exports rose by nearly 14 per cent. In each of these years though, GDP which had been growing at an annual real rate of 8 to 9 per cent since 1979 fell in 1982 (marginally) and by almost 5 per cent in 1983. The current position for Mexico appears to be favourable at the time of writing.

The same, however, cannot be said of Brazil, where the seeds of crisis were discussed in Chapter 3. The August 1982 announcement by Mexico acted in such a way as to damage yet further Brazil's access to external funds at that time. The current account deficit had reached 63 per cent of exports of goods and services and, with the Mexican development, Brazil was frozen out of financial markets. An emergency international support programme similar to that for Mexico was begun in December 1982, together with rescheduling of debt payments originally due during 1983.

In total value, the Brazilian emergency arrangements were $13.4

billion made up in a similar way to those for Mexico. Thus $4.6 billion came from the extended Fund facility over three years as well as $1.3 billion from the compensatory financing facility in the Fund. The IMF arrangements were made in January, whereas the United States had stepped in during the previous month. The US Treasury provided $1.53 billion as a ninety day loan. The European Central Banks provided (again through the BIS) $1.2 billion and the US Federal Reserve provided another bridging loan of $400 million.

Finally, again, the IMF insisted on rescheduling and an increase in bank exposure; this time to the amount of $4.4 billion, making up the total of the emergency package. The rescheduling agreement reached at the end of December, in addition to the new loans, included a rescheduling over eight years of $4 billion in principal originally payable in 1983. Short term trade credits were also to be maintained at their existing level ($8.8 billion) and, relating back to our discussion of the inter-bank market in Chapter 4, the final component was to return to the Brazilian banks' foreign branches the inter-bank deposit levels which had prevailed in mid 1982. The banks also provided immediate bridging finance in respect of the newly arranged loans mentioned.

What are the implications of such reschedulings for the banks? We consider the impact on earnings and on risk. In the two cases considered it is hard to argue that bank *earnings* were adversely affected. For Mexico, the rescheduling of its public debt involved 'spreads' over LIBOR of roughly 2.5 per cent, whereas loans negotiated between 1978 and 1980 averaged a spread of 0.9 per cent, implying an increase in annual interest payments of roughly $560 million (Cline, 1984, p. 81). In addition to fees on the rescheduling the *new* bank lending carried spreads of roughly 2⅛ per cent – almost two percentage points over the 1978–80 figure. The rise in rates was not so great for Brazil compared with its recent experience but the spreads over LIBOR were well in excess of 2 per cent.

These loan conditions eased somewhat for both countries in 1983 and most spectacular was the 'reward' for successful adjustment that was proposed for Mexico in late 1984. This represented the largest rescheduling to date, involving a total of $48.7 billion. Spreads were now down to around 1.1 per cent and a part of the rescheduling was due to take place without explicit IMF involvement (since the latter was to terminate during 1985). Evidently Mexico was well on the way to a recovery of commercial creditworthiness and the banks were optimistic that commercial funds should be available to the country in the late 1980s. This of course would be crucial to allow Mexico to 'roll over' the loans coming due under the rescheduled arrangements (Montagnon, 1984b).

How far does this experience imply that the earlier optimism of the banks towards sovereign lending risk had substance? The speed with which the international community reacted certainly suggests that prompt responses have been forthcoming to prevent major default. Similarly, for Brazil, although the adjustment has been a lot less smooth than that for Mexico, recent financial involvement by the multilateral institutions has broken new ground. For instance, a substantial role being played by the World Bank in effectively providing Brazil with extra, immediate, balance of payments support has been revealed (Whitley, 1984).

None the less, as Cline points out, and as the case study of Chapter 3 suggested, Brazil's financial future remains uncertain. Despite the reschedulings to date, Brazil has had repeated difficulty in maintaining the IMF-imposed fiscal and monetary targets. There is less scope for economy than Mexico had at the outset of its successful adjustment and the political feasibility of the current fiscal targets against the prospect of a newly elected civilian government is far from clear.

For the banks, the position is certainly that their loans are in each case 'tied up' for a considerable period and cannot be used for other purposes. Moreover should, say, Brazil's difficulties mount, pressure may also grow for solutions which would damage banks earnings after all. One possibility, which has already been raised, is that of interest capitalization in which due interest is added to the outstanding capital amount. For the banks, domestic regulators may well require that loans on which interest has been capitalized be classified as 'non-performing'. If also loan loss provisions were to be made against them both these and the disallowed interest accruals arising from non-performing status would damage bank profits very substantially.

More serious financial outcomes are conceivable. If countries were to announce moratoria for specific periods of time on their repayments of principal and interest, severe effects on bank profits could be expected. An example given by Cline (1984, p. 27) is that of Argentina, Brazil and Mexico jointly announcing such a moratorium for one year. On the assumption that these payments were written off by the banks, losses are calculated as equal to 28 per cent of the capital of the nine largest American banks. The ultimate loss, the write-off of the entire debt of one of the major borrowers, would be devastating. Citicorp's loans to Brazil, for example, represent around three-quarters of its issued capital and for Chase Manhattan the ratio is 57 per cent.

With figures such as these it is difficult to argue that the outcome of the process reviewed in this chapter has not been increased risk to the world's large banks. In order to take the analysis of the emergence of this condition further, however, the next chapter brings the focus to bear on the experience of the two banks just mentioned. How did they develop over the critical period of the 1970s and how, if at all, did they respond to the emerging risks we have discussed here?

NOTES

1 Goodman, whose terminology we are using, refers to 'fund availability' risk in this context if the withdrawal occurs simultaneously from a number of institutions.
2 *A Survey of Country Evaluation Systems in Use.* Export–Import Bank (United States). Details are summarized in Angelini *et a*.., 1979, pp. 122–4.
3 Perhaps the most influential of these is published annually by *Euromoney*. Each country's rank based on an index of the loan terms it achieved in all of its approaches to the market in that year:

$$\sum \frac{\text{Volume} \times \text{Spread} \times \text{Maturity}}{\text{Volume} \times \text{Maturity}}$$

with the summation being over the various loans to the country in the year. The index was later adjusted to allow for changing market conditions throughout the year:

$$\sum \frac{\text{Volume} \times \text{Spread}}{\text{Euromoney Index}} \Big/ \sum \text{Volume} \times \text{Maturity}.$$

In addition to syndications the index now incorporates bond issues and some other lending.

6 Bank balance sheet adjustment in a competitive environment

Factors behind the emergence of a substantial weight of individual country debt in bank balance sheets were discussed in the last chapter. When we come to consider the risks implied by this position for the continued operation of major lending banks the relationship between the composition of the institution's loan portfolio and the liabilities which fund it becomes critical. Particular attention, for instance, is drawn to the relationship between the size of loans to individual countries and the size of bank capital. Should default by the former threaten, through the losses written off, to eliminate the latter then the bank faces the real possibility of insolvency. Abstracting from the existence of other classes of debt, the implication of such an outcome would be of possible losses incurred by depositors.

Accordingly, the risks facing an individual bank depend on decisions taken on *both* sides of the balance sheet, in particular with respect to risk-bearing funds. The relationship between a bank's risks of insolvency, the composition of its loan portfolio, and the size of its share capital base can be neatly displayed in terms of the well-known mean-variance analysis of portfolio selection (Tobin, 1965). This approach distinguishes the mathematical expectation of return on an asset from the variability (variance) of those returns. The expectation is simply the range of rates of return which may be envisaged weighted by the subjective probabilities that each of those out-turns will occur. If, for instance, an investor believes there is an even chance of a rate of return being 20 per cent or 10 per cent, the mathematical expectation of return will be 15 per cent. The individual investor, however, is unlikely to be indifferent between this investment and a *certain* return of 15 per cent. Since the latter offers a definite return with zero variance, a risk-averse investor would prefer it to the former despite the even chance of a 20 per cent return on that investment. An investor of different psychology (a 'risk lover'), however, may well prefer to take the chance on a 20 per cent return.

More generally, given predominant risk aversion, an investment with a more widely spread range of possible outcomes (high variance) would require to produce a higher expectation of return than a safe (low variance) asset. Given two (or more) differing potential investments an important point arising is that a combined portfolio will usually offer a higher return for a given level of risk than a portfolio of only one asset. If the range of possible outcomes on each is (largely) uncorrelated, there is at least a chance that a negative outcome on one investment would be offset by a better than average outcome on the other. This can be depicted in the familiar opportunity locus of risk and return displayed in Figure 6.1, showing the combinations available as the shares of A and B vary in the portfolio. The mean expected return and its variance in the portfolio can be related to the risk of bank insolvency by the specification of a critical level of loss at which the bank's capital would be eliminated. The specification of a *given probability of bankruptcy* due to this event can be shown in the diagram as a ray from the critical loss (negative profits) level.

The rationale for the line is shown in Appendix A when the implication is that a steeper ray reflects a lower probability of bankruptcy. For any one portfolio selection (D in the figure) and level of bank capital (which sets the critical L), there is a given ray showing the probability of bankruptcy. Any point on the availabilities envelope to the left of DC implies a lower probability as the weight of B in the portfolio is reduced in favour of A.

Shown clearly by Figure 6.1, however, is the important point that the level of expected return as well as risk affects the probability of bankruptcy. Thus the probability with the safe portfolio C is identical with the riskier D. It is worth emphasizing at this point that, other things being equal, a higher co-variance of return on the assets A and B would imply higher bankruptcy risk for a given expected return in that the availability envelope would be flatter between A and B (Shapiro, 1982, p. 733).

The second clear implication of Figure 6.1 is that the only way for the bank to increase its expected returns above those provided by D, without at the same time increasing bankruptcy risk, would be by increasing the level of bank capital. In terms of Figure 6.1, this would permit the rightward parallel shift of the ray as the level of tolerable losses would increase. Even from the shareholders' point of view it may be argued that bank capital has the important role of permitting the bank to hold a higher expected return portfolio without increasing the probability of the extraordinary costs associated with the actual or potential bankruptcy of the institution. This, as Baltensperger has pointed out, is fundamentally similar to the function of liquidity reserves in helping to prevent extraordinary losses attendant on the forced sale of illiquid assets if such reserves (or capital) were to appear

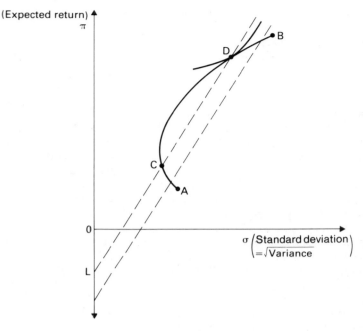

Figure 6.1

inadequate during banking operations (Baltensperger, 1980, p. 11). In terms of extraordinary costs, of course, the higher the social cost of bank failure the higher would the authorities be likely to set the required capital levels. Interestingly, deliberate interference with the choice of assets which a bank is allowed to hold (especially the banning of certain assets) would not substitute for inadequate capital. Such regulations, by shifting the availabilities envelope down to the right, could well increase the probability of bank failure (Blair and Heggestad, 1979).

From the point of view of avoiding insolvency then, there is an obvious rationale for share capital to receive enhanced emphasis in funding as the loan portfolio becomes both more potentially profitable and risky. At this stage, however, a fundamental issue emerges concerning bank risk and the interests to which management are required to respond. This concerns the possibility of conflict between the interests of shareholders (which are usually assumed to be of paramount importance in the eyes of management) and other constituencies including deposit holders, regulatory authorities, and financial markets generally. The possible source of conflict is implied in the modern theory of capital asset pricing which emphasizes the need to distinguish between 'firm-specific' and 'systematic' risk. Not surprisingly, firm-specific risks arise as a result of the operations and decisions of a particular firm which, in our context, would include the particular borrowing and lending decisions of a bank. Systematic risks on the other hand are those which impinge on firms in general such as developments in the level of macro-economic activity. The contention of the capital asset pricing model is that, with efficient capital markets, firm-specific risk can be 'diversified away'. For instance, shareholders in one firm (or bank) can insure themselves against the risks specific to those shares by holding a diversified portfolio. On the other hand, if the expected returns co-vary positively with the variance of return to companies in general, then the value of portfolio diversification is much reduced – a worse than expected outcome on one share being associated with a negative result on the others (e.g. Mossin, 1969).

The relevance of this for present purposes is that the various risks we have so far discussed will pertain to the assets and liabilities of a particular bank, and possibly to the small number of major multinational banks as well. A widely diversified portfolio of shares should much reduce the shareholder's concern with these particular risks. His main concern is with the mathematical expectation of return. If this concern predominates in the eyes of management, expected profit maximization, not risk aversion would be the main objective.[1]

Clearly, however, shareholders are not the only constituency to be considered. Whereas they may be willing to accept loss on one component of a diversified portfolio, bank deposits are generally regarded by their owners as low risk liquid resources. On this understanding, failure of a bank in which those deposits were vested would be a different matter from the point of view of the depositor. It would in fact imply that he had been an unwilling 'shareholder' in a risky asset portfolio without the attendant *ex ante* privilege of a share in possible profits. Given perfect capital markets, where ignorance may be assumed away, or at least perfect competition among financial intermediaries, such depositor misfortune would not occur (Fama, 1980). In Fama's outline of a purely competitive intermediation (banking) system, financial intermediaries would justify their existence by offering depositors access to an accounting system of exchange (permitting, for example, the service of cheque clearing) and by acting as portfolio managers. In this last capacity it is frequently assumed that financial intermediaries take advantage of certain 'economies of scale' in managing asset (loan) portfolios not possessed by individual depositors should they wish to lend directly to ultimate borrowers (e.g. Gurley and Shaw, 1960, p. 194). A bank, or other intermediary, therefore would be able to earn a higher return for a given level of portfolio risk than could an individual maintaining his own portfolio. On this basis, Fama's model suggests that intermediaries would offer a variety of portfolios with differing levels of risk and return and potential depositors would choose according to their own preferences. Accordingly depositors, in return for higher interest earnings, would accept the risks of loss on the portfolio in which they effectively had a share.

Given the probability that there would exist a demand for 'riskless' deposits the perfectly competitive banking system could cater in two ways. Firstly, banks could offer one portfolio consisting of riskless assets; for instance, short term securities with fixed redemption value. Secondly, and more reflective of real world circumstances, the bank could offer a common diversified portfolio (with components of more or less risk) and offer differing classes of deposits against it. One class may be riskless *provided that there were sufficient holders of other knowingly risky deposits for their funds always to be sufficient to absorb any potential losses on the portfolio* (Fama, 1980, p. 42). As Fama suggests, this would be similar to the real world relationship between a bank's supposed risk-free deposit categories and its shareholders. It is the latter's resources which should bear any potential portfolio losses. In Fama's model various classes of depositors are fully aware of the risks being taken on their behalf and, since these would be reflected competitively in risk-adjusted interest payments, the banks' profits would be determined entirely by portfolio management fees, again competitively determined. There would be no way for the bank to improve its overall returns by offering to the public differing mixes of deposit types. The system would conform to the fundamental Modigliani–Miller proposition that the returns to any firm (and thereby its overall market value) are determined entirely by the return on its assets and are quite independent of the way it chooses to finance them.

Under what circumstances then may shareholder interests run counter to those of depositors? Taggart and Greenbaum (1978) develop a relevant argument by recognizing that in a non-regulated situation, and compatible with the Modigliani–Miller thesis, deposit interest rates would include a risk premium related to the probability of bankruptcy. Accordingly the advantage of raising more equity capital is twofold. First, it reduces the risk of depositor losses in the event of unsuccessful trading, but secondly, by so doing it reduces the deposit interest rates that the bank is called upon to pay. This in turn benefits the shareholders' expected returns provided that profitable lending opportunities exist. If banking regulations are now introduced into this environment, the optimal deposit–equity mix implied by the model (where marginal cost of equity is equated to the incremental returns described) will be disturbed.

An important intervention pointing in the direction of deposit rather than equity financing is the phenomenon of deposit insurance. The existence of such bodies as the Federal Deposit Insurance Corporation (FDIC) in the USA effectively protects certain classes of deposit from the effects of bank failure. In terms of the Taggart–Greenbaum model, such a system breaks the link between deposit interest rates and bankruptcy risk. As these authors assume that profits are made from the transactions services associated with deposits, the incentive to raise share capital is very much weakened by the insurance scheme since shareholders reap the benefit of low cost deposit funds as 'gearing' increases.

Although only a minority of deposits are explicitly covered by the FDIC, it is not unreasonable to suggest that (for instance) international agreements between central banks lessen the *perceived* risk of depositor loss in all categories and indirectly reduce the cost of deposit funds to the banks. This unintended incentive may well increase the actual risks faced by non-insured depositors and the 'moral hazard' problem for regulatory authorities seeking to increase the safety of the international banking system. Accordingly the authorities would be expected to impose on bank management a concern with total (systematic and firm-specific) risk (Shapiro, 1982). However, prior to explicit regulatory requirements being imposed on bank portfolio or share capital decisions, in a situation where deposit costs are insensitive to portfolio risk, such risks must be assessed by management.[2] This in turn raises the possibility that risk assessment will become much influenced by the competitive environment, particularly given the interests of shareholders which we have noted. This point, which may help to provide further explanation of the growing importance of country lending during the period, and the optimism with which it was viewed, is developed later in the chapter.

The foregoing review of factors underlying the probability of bank failure has sought to emphasize the role of the entire asset portfolio along with the structure of liabilities. To assess developments in these areas, in the practical context of international banking, the discussion will now turn to an examination of the evolution of the asset and liability structures of two leading international banks, Citicorp and the Chase Manhattan Corporation. These institutions are chosen simply because they are representative of major banks with highly developed international business and evidence on changing bank balance sheet structure is presented in two stages. Overall developments between 1972 and 1981 are first reported followed by a consideration of annual changes in order to assess the year on year evenness of the

Table 6.1　Citicorp: summary average balance sheet data 1972–81

	1972 $ (millions)	1972 Composition (%)	1981 $ (millions)	1981 Composition (%)	Growth rate
Assets					
Cash at interest with banks	3,042	10.2	13,067	11.3	18.5
Investment securities	3,032	10.1	6,927	6.0	
Trading account	264	0.9	2,596	2.2	
Federal funds sold u.r.a.	103	0.3	2,555	2.2	
Total	6,441		25,145		
Loans and lease					
Domestic offices	10,632	35.5	30,193	26.0	9.4
Overseas offices	8,193	27.4	41,833	36.1	18.5
Direct lease	313	1.0	1,851	1.6	
Total loans and lease	19,143		73,877		
Non-interest-bearing assets	4,358	14.6	16,873	14.6	12.9
Total assets	29,942	100.0	115,895	100.0	14.5
Liabilities					
Deposits					
Demand	6,586	22.0	8,615	7.4	1.7
Savings and time	6,455	21.6	11,384	9.8	3.1
Overseas offices	11,477	38.3	52,132	45.0	17.1
Total deposits	24,518		72,131		

Table 6.1 (*continued*)

Interest-bearing funds					
Federal funds purchased u.r.a.	1,277	4.3	10,936	9.4	23.9
Other borrowed money	832	2.8	14,492	12.5	30.1
Total interest-bearing funds	2,109		25,428		
Non-interest bearing funds	1,561	5.2	10,733	9.3	
Intermediate debt	101	0.3	922	0.8	
Long term notes	154	0.5	2,654	2.3	
(1) Total liabilities	28,443		111,868		14.6
(2) Shareholders' equity	1,499	5.0 (5.6)	4,027	3.5 (4.0)	10.3
Total 1 + 2	29,942	100.0	115,895	100.0	14.5

developments outlined. Following the empirical review, an interpretation in terms of the risk factors discussed above will be attempted. This exercise will be supported by reference to a formal model of bank balance sheet adjustment in the face of risky lending. The model is developed in Appendix B.

CHANGING BALANCE SHEET STRUCTURE: THE EVIDENCE 1972-81

A preliminary investigation is provided in Tables 6.1 and 6.2. Here the broad balance sheet categories are depicted together with the (semi-log) trend rates of growth of the most significant items. Since these vary, the balance sheet structures have changed between the two years chosen. A discussion of changes in the structure of bank balance sheets, however, has to recognize their somewhat peculiar nature in comparison with the accounts of non-financial firms. The balance sheet is usually interpreted as a statement of the position of the enterprise on the accounting date, and as such the values are seen in terms of a stock concept. For the bank balance sheet, however, we are dealing with 'financial' rather than 'real' magnitudes which are continuously turning over as loans are repaid and deposits refinanced. The banker is able to reassess the composition of his stock of assets and liabilities, therefore, on a continuous basis. The implication of this is that the annual 'snapshot' of the bank's position may show very considerable variation without the implication that this reflects changes of substance over the twelve month period (Sealey and Lindley, 1977, p. 1254). Accordingly, the data presented are annual average values.

Quantitatively, the most significant development on the assets side for both institutions has been the shift in emphasis from domestic to foreign lending. The latter has increasingly dominated the activity of these banks, sustaining the nominal growth of their balance sheets in the face of slow domestic expansion. It also represents a continuation of the trend to foreign business which emerged in the 1960s under the impetus of financing the overseas expansion of US-based multinational firms (Pringle, 1966). At the beginning of the 1970s, however, the growth was increasingly affected by the emergence of syndicated lending based on 'roll-over' credits. This technical development increased both the feasibility and the attraction of bank participation in large loans, including those to foreign governments. It is interesting to note that these developments preceded by several years the first oil crisis (e.g. Galbraith, 1971) and that anxiety over the soundness of some lending was being expressed also at an early stage (The Banker, 1971).

Indeed, the same article refers to the connection between syndicated lending and the banks' belief that they would permit reduced liquidity margins without a decline in soundness of operations. There is a hint of the connection between the expansion of overseas lending and liquidity margins on the assets side of the balance sheets we are considering. In the case of Citicorp, overseas and domestic lending reverse their relative weights in the balance sheet between the two years shown with the total level of lending (domestic and overseas) representing a constant fraction. For Chase Manhattan total lending rises to a comparable fraction of almost two-thirds by 1981. This expansion is entirely the result of growing foreign lending.

For both banks, the contrast on the assets side is the declining relative position of 'investment securities'. As these represent the banks' portfolio holdings of Federal and State government securities, together with certain municipal bonds, they are also a relatively liquid or marketable asset. Again, in the 1960s regulatory fears were expressed over the declining proportion of total bank lending represented by these assets (e.g. Beckhart, 1972, p. 349). The 'trading account securities' mentioned also include government stocks but represents a much more volatile item as this account is specifically used for day to day trading and the securities are shown in the balance sheet at market value. The liquid asset item which has increased its relative balance sheet proportion in the case of both banks is that of cash deposits at overseas banks and are representative, therefore, of the growing amounts of inter-bank business referred to in Chapter 4. The underlying growth rate of this item has certainly been higher than that of the balance sheet totals. In this context, it may be mentioned that non-interest-bearing cash reserves are included in the item 'non-interest-bearing assets' which also includes customers' acceptance liabilities.

From the point of view of bank assets therefore, the growing importance of overseas lending, in contrast with the modest expansion of domestic loan business, has accompanied a relative shift of more liquid assets away from government securities in favour of loans to overseas banks. The impression gained here is that the relatively rapid expansion of overseas lending has not been matched by the expansion of liquid assets as a whole. This observation, in turn, throws into relief the importance, which the banks themselves stress, of 'liability management' as a means of funding their loan business. In this connection we may consider the various liability items shown.

As with the loan breakdown, the most impressive development has been in the relative importance of domestic and foreign deposits. For

Table 6.2   Chase Manhattan: summary average balance sheet data 1972–81

	1972		1981		
	$ (millions)	Composition (%)	$ (millions)	Composition (%)	Growth rate
Assets					
Cash at interest with banks	2,631	9.7	8,725	11.5	15.3
Investment securities	2,999	11.0	4,318	5.7	
Trading account securities	420	1.5	318	0.4	
Federal funds sold u.r.a.	70	0.3	607	0.8	
Total	6,120		13,968		
Loans					
Domestic offices	11,374	41.7	19,882	26.3	4.9
Overseas offices	3,685	13.5	27,752	36.7	24.9
Total loans	15,059		47,634		
Non-interest-bearing assets	6,080	22.3	13,977	18.5	
Total assets	27,259	100.0	75,579	99.9	10.8
Liabilities					
Deposits					
Demand	8,537	31.3	11,391	15.1	2.4
Savings and time	5,728	21.0	12,190	16.1	8.3
Overseas offices	7,662	28.1	31,998	42.3	16.7
Total deposits	21,927		55,579		

Table 6.2 (continued)

Interest-bearing funds					
Federal funds purchased u.r.a.	1,378	5.1	4,708	6.2	17.0
Other borrowed money	361	1.3	5,050	6.7	24.1
Total interest-bearing funds	1,739		9,758		
Non-interest bearing funds	1,533	5.6	5,986	7.9	
Long term notes	528	1.9	963	1.3	
(1) Total liabilities	25,727		72,286		11.0
(2) Shareholders' equity	1,532	5.6	3,293	4.4	7.0
Total 1 + 2	27,259	100	75,579	100.0	10.8

(1) Items may not sum to 100 due to rounding

both banks, the contribution to the balance sheet of both domestic deposit classes shown has declined. By comparison with these the growth of overseas deposits has been such that they represented in excess of 40 per cent of the balance sheet total in the later year. Again, the growth rate of these overseas funds has been well in excess of the growth of total business. Even so, total deposits have not kept pace with this growth, implying for both banks a significant deterioration in the total loans : total deposits ratio.

A major determinant of this increased dependence on overseas funds is to be found in the acute 'financial repression' occasioned by domestic American banking legislation. Thus, 'Regulation Q' (the phasing out of which was commenced in March 1980 by the Monetary Control Act) imposed ceilings on the interest rates payable on domestic time deposits. The inflationary conditions of the 1970s meant that these ceilings increasingly represented negative real rates of interest. At the same time non-bank intermediaries not covered by Regulation Q were increasingly offering more attractive services to savers. Instances of this trend were the negotiated order of withdrawal (NOW) accounts initially offered by savings and loan associations and the money market funds developed by securities firms. Both offered combinations of interest and liquidity which the regulated banks were unable to match. Similar influences were at work on the demand deposit base since no offset to inflation losses were possible through interest payments (Berger, 1981).

Not only was new, non-regulated, competition stimulated by domestic inflation, but legislation also impeded the competitive response normally seen when interest rate controls apply. Thus, the McFadden Act, which is the fundamental law intended to prevent inter-state banking, is only being slowly eroded through the operation of the Bank Holding Companies Act of 1965. The ability to establish deposit-seeking branches across state boundaries was therefore constrained, but even more restrictive has been the prevention *within* many states of branch banking. Only after 1976, for instance, was branch banking permitted throughout New York State. The proliferation of branches as a means of attracting depositors, together with undercharging for banking services (to compensate interest rate ceilings), has consequently been inhibited.

In marked contrast to this complex legislative environment the ability of overseas branches to attract deposits has been completely unfettered by either reserve requirements or interest rate ceilings. The results of this freedom are manifested in the balance sheet figures shown in Tables 6.1 and 6.2.

A fundamental problem for the banks as a consequence of these conditions has been the need to obtain funds to service their business when the traditional routes for doing so have been partially blocked. Active 'liability management' has led to the development of new debt instruments partly to circumvent controls. On the deposit side, for instance, the emergence of negotiable certificates of deposit (CDs) was an early innovation by Citicorp. Since interest payments were not permitted on deposits of less than thirty days, CDs were written for thirty days or longer with most maturing in ninety days or less. However, since these certificates are negotiable, the holder need not keep them for this period, but may sell them in a secondary market. Such instruments have been a particularly important component of the growth of time and savings deposits depicted in the balance sheets. Nevertheless, as the growth rates are unadjusted for inflation, domestic deposit expansion has clearly been slow.

The second interesting feature of the liabilities shown is the increasingly active use made of the two items listed under 'interest-bearing funds'. 'Federal funds purchased and securities sold under repurchase arrangements' represents two types of transaction. Federal funds purchased represent borrowings by the banks of the excess cash reserves of other member banks of the Federal Reserve system where excess is in respect of legally stipulated minima. As such, the borrowings are of very short maturity reflecting variations in the daily reserve position and, indeed, an important reason for the existence of the market is that whereas cheques drawn on a Reserve bank are *immediately* credited to the holder, cheques drawn on other commercial banks are credited to the holder bank after a delay. As reserve deficiencies attract a penalty there is incentive to borrow (at interest) these 'instantaneous' funds to cover a threatened deficiency. It has traditionally been the case that the net suppliers of funds to the market have been the smaller domestic banks with excess reserves, whereas the largest net users have been the major 'money centre' institutions. These transactions are, in principle, unsecured, whereas the second type of operation, 'securities sold under repurchase arrangements' represent borrowings against the collateral of subgroups of 'investment securities'. That is the borrowing bank will acquire funds by selling some securities with an agreement to buy them back at a specified future date. The repurchase price would include an interest component (Beckhart, 1972, pp. 71–75). Again, the bulk of these transactions have an overnight maturity (Weberman, 1972, p. 1683), but it is clear from the balance sheet amounts in our two examples that the contribution of these funds has grown rapidly, with an average annual nominal rate of growth of 17–24 per cent. In the first case the weight in the balance sheet has doubled by 1981 (to 9.4 per cent).

Even more rapid growth may be seen to have occurred in the second category of interest-bearing funds, 'other borrowed money'. In the published accounts these are seen to comprise 'commercial paper' as well as 'other borrowed funds', with the latter largely originating overseas. 'Commercial paper' has been another highly active area of liability management. Essentially representing promissory notes, the extension of use of these instruments had been rapid in 1969 during the credit contraction of that year. The Federal Reserve was then of the opinion that the expansion of their use represented a threat to the operation of monetary control policies (Beckhart, 1972, p. 406). Accordingly, during 1970 the same reserve requirements as those applied to deposits were applied to these funds. Depending on the controls being exercised at any one moment, this type of paper has been substitutable for CDs from the liability management point of view (Beckhart, 1972).

Taking the 'other borrowed money' category as one the annual growth rate has been between 24 and 30 per cent, a substantial growth even when inflation is accounted for. Indeed, in both cases, but most noticeably in the case of Citicorp, these funds, together with 'Federal funds purchased' have substantially compensated for the failure of total deposits to keep in step with the growth of overall business.

A final noteworthy point on the liabilities side, for both banks, has been the continuing, though marginal, deterioration in the debt : equity ratio. This is clear whether or not we include loan loss provisions (a non-cash expense) as part of shareholders' funds. The bracketed figures for Citicorp make this adjustment whereas the figures for Chase Manhattan are already so expressed. Given the initial small ratios involved the equity fraction of total liabilities has declined significantly, although there is a necessary caveat here. There exists the possibility of 'hidden' or 'secret' reserves, though perhaps the most obvious way of creating these would be by overstated loan loss provisions which are already covered by their allocation to shareholders' funds. No other explicit reserves are set aside by these banks but scope for them exists and, in the UK, they have been expressly permitted for banks as a means of avoiding sudden changes in the reported accounts. This in turn is justified on the grounds of maintenance of 'confidence' in the institutions concerned. It is possible, for instance, that banks would wish to use such provisions to maintain a steady flow of dividend payments when the current profit position may not warrant it. There is no reason to believe, however, that even if such reserves did exist (despite announced policy to the contrary) the situation would be much altered.

Accepting the published figures, therefore, the decline in shareholders' funds as a proportion of total liabilities appears to have occurred in similar measure for both banks.

A reasonable conclusion to draw from the declining equity ratio, and consistent with frequent assertions, is that share capital has been a relatively expensive form of financing for the banks. Certainly common stock issues have been very small indeed with the growth in shareholders' equity coming substantially from retained earnings. Indeed some insight into retention policy may be gained from the following estimated equations of dividend behaviour.

These equations suggest that only between 20–30 per cent of annual income is declared as dividends, a figure supported by wider studies of US banks (e.g. Mayne, 1980). Additionally, there is some weak support for the hypothesis that dividends tend to be constrained by the need for capital to maintain pace with asset growth. However, the negative sign on the last variable is highly tentative given the failure of the estimated coefficients to reach the 10 per cent level of significance.[3]

The reliance on different forms of debt financing has recently been highlighted by the criticism which these and other major US banks have faced over the financing decisions of their parent companies. Under the Bank Holding Company Act of 1965, holding companies have been able to issue long term debt, employing the funds raised to purchase equity in their bank subsidiaries. This practice has led to the allegation of double leveraging since much of this debt is subordinated to that of the bank subsidiary in the event of insolvency claims. As a consequence, such debt becomes somewhat akin to an equity investment in the banking business. It is possible, for instance, that if the banking business were to become unprofitable, the holding company's position might be threatened, given debt service

Table 6.3 *Estimated dividend functions: Chase Manhattan and Citicorp*

Chase 1969–81		
	$D = 39{,}268.4 + 0.2198\,Y - 361.62\Delta A,$ $\quad\quad\quad\quad (10.742)\quad (1.053)$	$R^2 = 0.905$
Citicorp 1972–81		
	$D = 12{,}590.5 + 0.2937\,Y - 170.46\Delta A,$ $\quad\quad\quad\quad (8.253)\quad\quad (0.332)$	$R^2 = 0.904$

Definitions: D, annual cash dividends declared; Y, income before securities gains and losses; ΔA, annual percentage growth rates of average assets; t-ratios are shown in parentheses.

Notes: (a) The definition of income chosen is dictated by the apparent obligation to capitalize income from gains on securities transactions (Mayne, 1980). (b) *Average* asset growth was chosen as a more reliable indicator of underlying expansion than year on year balance sheet figures.

commitments. Fears of this nature led to an explicit downgrading of the credit ratings of most of the major US bank holding companies by both Moody's and Standard and Poors. Downgrading of Citicorp by Standard and Poors occurred in September 1981 and by Moody's in January 1982, with that company being heavily criticized for the practice mentioned. Thus a large part of the $2.8 billion of long term debt noted in the balance sheet for 1981 was debt of the parent company (approximately $1.8 billion).

The nature of the 'signals' sent by financial markets to bank management concerning perceptions of the degree of risk faced by the individual institution will be briefly raised below when the balance sheet data are interpreted. Before this exercise is undertaken, however, a further look at the data on an annual basis could be revealing. To what extent have the structural changes between the beginning and end of our period of study reflected a smooth transition over the years? Is there any evidence, on the other hand, that managements have sought to moderate these changes over time?

To provide insight into such questions annual changes in balance sheet structure require to be depicted, and we use below the information theory techniques first applied to accounting data by Theil (1968). This approach allows a single summary measure of the deviation from proportionality exhibited between two balance sheets, weighting each deviation by its relative importance in the overall statement. As the measure is based on logarithms to base 2, the units are 'bits' of information. The larger the value the more the balance sheet has deviated from proportionality between the beginning and end of the year.

Tables 6.4 and 6.5 present the assets and liabilities information. Considering assets first the 'base ratio' reported is a summary of deviation from proportional change in the categories depicted in Tables 6.1 and 6.2 above without the breakdown of the 'loans and lease' category. Using the additive property of the logarithm measure the weighted deviation of the loans and lease category is reported separately, with the third column giving the 'aggregate breakdown'. The latter, being the sum of the first two, is the information index for the assets side, including variations within the 'loans and lease' category. In the case of Table 6.5 the 'base ratio' again represents the deviations from proportional change for the categories reported in Tables 6.1 and 6.2 without a decomposition of the various types of deposits. A peculiarity on the liabilities side is that the category of total shareholders' funds is unlikely to show as much variation as the other liabilities. Accordingly, the base ratio is broken down into the variation from proportionality for shareholders' funds *vis-à-vis* total non-shareholder liabilities and the weighted deviation of the various

Table 6.4   *Assets information decomposition (10⁻⁶ bits): Chase Manhattan (A) and Citicorp (B)*

	Base ratio		+	Loans		=	Aggregate breakdown	
	A	B		A	B		A	B
1972/3	12,144	8,300		11,708	5		23,852	8,305
1973/4	3,688	6,882		7,483	1,196		11,171	8,078
1974/5	15,593	6,348		2,509	8,945		18,102	15,294
1975/6	4,463	2,158		4,534	9,613		8,997	11,770
1976/7	602	15,825		5,907	3,810		6,509	19,636
1977/8	4,104	5,518		4,518	178		8,622	5,696
1978/9	788	5,514		109	651		897	6,165
1979/80	1,520	4,852		469	2,033		1,989	6,886
1980/1	2,550	5,832		219	654		2,769	6,486

types of non-capital liabilities within the total liabilities (less shareholders' funds). The additional variation within the deposits category is reported separately.

The overall impression gained from the asset and liability decompositions is of greater variability in the years to 1976–7 than in the subsequent period. This inference appears valid for both banks on the asset side as the 'aggregate breakdown' of Table 6.4 makes clear. Although less clear for liabilities, the major liability composition changes for Citicorp do seem to have occurred in the years to 1976–7. A major shift also occurs in this case during 1978–9. Considering the composition of deposit liabilities (essentially the location at domestic

Table 6.5   *Liability information decomposition (10⁻⁶ bits): Chase Manhattan (A) and Citicorp (B)*

	Base ratio		=	SK/ liabilities		+	Liabilities		Deposits	
	A	B		A	B		A	B	A	B
1972/3	10,401	10,116		476	166		9,925	9,951	7,286	1,897
1973/4	4,883	18,621		888	808		3,994	17,813	6,233	2,717
1974/5	1,133	14,663		186	0		947	14,663	1,458	4,448
1975/6	879	2,413		28	194		851	2,219	5,757	6,402
1976/7	322	8,951		57	84		265	8,867	4,093	12,226
1977/8	2,419	4,375		20	121		2,399	4,254	4,318	1,353
1978/9	2,045	15,433		3	120		2,042	15,313	2,600	3,667
1979/80	498	4,990		4	19		494	4,971	2,258	531
1980/1	313	2,548		19	1		294	2,547	5,810	2,572

SK, total shareholders' funds.

Table 6.6   *Trend nominal growth rates of selected assets and liabilities (per cent per annum): Chase Manhattan*

Liabilities	1972–7	1977–81	Assets	1972–7	1977–81
Deposits					
Demand	1.7	5.6	Cash at		
Savings/time	6.9	9.8	interest	10.4	12.7
Foreign	17.8	11.8			
Total	10.0	9.9			
Short term			*Loans*		
funds			Domestic	4.1	8.6
Federal funds	13.9	11.4	Foreign	27.2	14.0
Other borrowed			Total	13.0	11.7
money	28.1	20.6			
Total	18.2	15.6			
Total liabilities	10.9	11.3			
Shareholders'					
funds	6.3	11.2			
Total liabilities/					
assets	10.7	11.3		10.7	11.3

and foreign offices) the main variations are concentrated in the period prior to 1976–7, as are the similar loans variations on the assets side.

To illuminate the content of these decomposition measures Tables 6.6 and 6.7 contrast (semi-log) trend growth rates suggested for the subperiods 1972–7 and 1977–81.

Although the suggested underlying growth rates must be taken as highly tentative given the small number of observations for each subperiod, some parallels with the decomposition analyses of Tables 6.4 and 6.5 are suggested. The growth rate data for Chase Manhattan suggest for both deposit and loan classifications a tendency to move towards the overall assets–liabilities growth rate. The most striking feature in each case is the slowing down of foreign activity much more towards the growth of the balance sheet in the second subperiod. Both domestic deposit categories along with domestic loans in turn move up towards the overall figure. Although total (non-capital) liabilities grow at a similar rate in both subperiods, shareholders funds grow at a rate comparable in the second period. Finally, the rate of growth of short term borrowing appears to slacken towards the overall growth performance. These trends are consistent with the apparent stabilization of balance sheet structure suggested by the decomposition analysis of Tables 6.4 and 6.5 for this institution. The behaviour of Citicorp seems, however, to be more complex. Much the same slackening of foreign business on the deposits and loans side is also witnessed here, suggesting again that these growth rates were beginning to come into line with the growth of overall business in the later years.

Table 6.7 *Trend nominal growth rates of selected assets and liabilities (per cent per annum): Citicorp*

Liabilities	1972-7	1977-81	Assets	1972-7	1977-81
Deposits					
Demand	4.2	2.2	Cash at		
Time/savings	5.6	5.3	interest	24.8	4.9
Foreign	22.0	10.1			
Total	14.7	8.2			
Short term funds			*Loans*		
			Domestic	5.4	19.3
Federal funds	18.9	28.0	Foreign	24.0	11.7
Other borrowed money	23.8	38.7	Total	15.6	14.5
Total	21.1	33.2			
Total liabilities	16.2	13.8			
Shareholders' funds	12.4	9.4			
Total liabilities/ assets	16.0	13.6		16.0	13.6

Moreover, on the loans side, there is a substantial increase suggested for domestic lending which even exceeds the growth rate of the total balance sheet. For Citicorp, however, there appears to be a continuing change into the later period in the composition of liabilities. There is no significant change in the growth of domestic deposit categories, unlike the previous case, and contrary to any slackening of expansion the growth rates suggest an increasing degree of reliance on the two categories of short term funds depicted. These trends again appear to be broadly consistent with the decomposition data in Tables 6.4 and 6.5. Indeed the large liability decomposition value displayed in Table 6.5 for 1978-9 is substantially attributable to a sharp increase in the use of short term funds and a *decline* in both domestic deposit categories. While these declines were marginal in nominal terms, the use of Federal funds expanded by 71 per cent, taking this category of borrowing to rough parity with the domestic demand deposit base. Other borrowed short term funds expanded by 51 per cent so that in 1979 this category exceeded the total of domestic savings and time deposits.

In another apparent contrast with the previous bank there is no sign of an increase in the rate of growth of shareholders' funds in the second subperiod. This difference, however, is possibly not as clear since Citicorp appears to have relied more heavily on the issue of long term notes, to which previous reference has been made. Annual reports also make clear that this has been the intended policy.

Emerging from the analysis, however, is a distinct tendency for the foreign-based component of both deposits and loans to show a reduced rate of growth of similar magnitude in the second subperiod along with some increase in domestic lending activity.

Before proceeding to an interpretation of these developments the increasingly important role of short term funding in these balance sheets deserves emphasis. How do such funds relate to the growth of foreign-based borrowing and lending which has been such a dominating feature in our examination? One possible interpretation would be based on the assumption that the making of (overseas) loans occurs prior to the receipt of (overseas) deposits. Since both show similar growth in the balance sheet data the alternative possibility that deposits lead loans cannot be ruled out. Indeed, the growth of deposits has sometimes been argued to be the major cause of the increase of sovereign lending in the 1970s. However, if deposits had been received before loans were made then *net liquid assets* would be expected to increase in the event of an upsurge of deposits such as occurred after the oil price increases. Both of the banks under review publish annual average and year end balance sheet information and there is little evidence from these that net liquid assets did rise during the years in which this might have been expected.

Perhaps a stronger reason for the belief that loans are extended prior to the receipt of deposits derives from the behaviour of borrowers in the market for *wholesale* loans. Kindleberger (1981) has drawn attention to the point that *assurance of supply of funds* when required is as important for the borrower as are considerations of the interest rate charged. Thus, a borrower facing the prospect of an enhanced need for funds (as in the case of countries anticipating the balance of payments costs of higher oil prices) would arrange lines of credit before they were actually needed. In this event, bank loans and deposits would tend to rise together with banks bidding for bulk deposits to finance their level of business. Bridging liquidity could be provided by their ready access to short term money markets. In fact there is a little evidence of substitutability between short term funds and bulk (overseas) deposits if this chain of events is accepted. The following equations report the results of regressing the average level of overseas deposits (OD) on the average level of overseas loans (OL) and the 'spread' (S) between the overseas deposit rate and the Federal funds rate as an indicator of the price of short term finance:

Chase Manhattan, 1969–81

$$OD = 3869.6 + 1.028\ OL - 255.4\ S, \qquad R^2 = 0.99;$$
$$(54.75) (1.64)$$

Citicorp, 1972–81

$$OD = 1691.2 + 1.235\ OL - 549.9\ S, \qquad R^2 = 0.99.$$
$$(48.25) (1.6)$$

(NB: t-ratios are given in parentheses.)

As these are nominal values the extremely strong correlation between overseas deposits and overseas loans, as suggested by reported 't' ratios in each case, is not surprising. Despite this, however, the 'spread' variable provides the predicted sign with a coefficient significant at better than the 10 per cent level. That is, there is some evidence here that overseas deposits have been bid for somewhat less strongly, given lending decisions, when short term interest rates have been comparatively low. This interpretation, if correct, suggests an initial willingness by the banks to participate in substantial lending on the basis of access to short term liquid funds later refinanced in the form of wholesale deposits. It is interesting to note at this point that the active liability management implied suggests that domestic monetary policy conditions (e.g. as depicted by the Federal funds rate) would have an almost immediate impact on the terms attached to overseas loans. As bulk deposit rates will respond to increased bids by banks seeking to reduce their use of short term funds the rate to final borrowers will reflect the changed circumstances.

If it is reasonable to assume that the demand for loans from overseas borrowers has 'driven' the expansion in overseas business, what can we conclude from the apparent change in patterns of balance sheet development following 1977? The most conspicuous element here, it will be recalled, was a movement away for disproportionate growth (relative to total assets) of overseas lending.

AN INTERPRETATION: RISK AND COMPETITION

Interpretation depends on the assumed objectives of management and the assumption here is one of *expected profit maximization*. This, as already noted, would reflect shareholder interests and is consistent with the high degree of response by the banks to changing circumstances in the 1970s. New areas of lending were argued to be highly lucrative and managements were judged and compared in financial markets by returns achieved on invested funds. Our earlier discussion suggested that, in so far as higher expected returns implied higher risk, one constraint on the profit-maximizing process would be the risk premia demanded by depositors on their funds, at least in an environment of pure competition.

In practice, a close functional relationship between risk and deposit interest rates has not been in evidence over the period concerned. Major American banks of the type studied trade in the wholesale deposit market (CDs) as a group ('on the run') with commonly quoted rates. Occasionally, members of the run have experienced adverse sentiment and have withdrawn temporarily, but they generally have access to the market on favourable terms. Markets such as that for CDs, however, do give some signals concerning the riskiness of banks. The market is clearly 'tiered', reflecting the stature of participating institutions with the most prestigious names able to command the finest terms. Secondly, in the aggregate, the CD rate has moved relative to the risk-free (e.g. Treasury Bill) rate following major banking 'scares' (Carron, 1982). The market experience of Manufacturers Hanover is a recent example of a widening of the 'spread' between CD and Treasury Bill rates (Financial Times, 1984).

This suggests that in maximizing profits managements have to take a view on levels of risk acceptable in such markets. However, even if explicit or implicit deposit insurance made depositor response to bank-specific risk unlikely, lending policies which increased the probability of bank failure would imply an increase in *potential* costs. Bankruptcy, whether actual or threatened, involves extraordinary costs of adjustment as, for instance, assets are liquidated at unfavourable terms in an attempt to stave off the event. Given these potential costs and their tendency to increase as the probability of failure rises, the expected return to the shareholder, which is being maximized, becomes sensitive to the risks which the bank is running (Baltensperger, 1980).

If risk is a source of potential cost, how might sources of increasing risk be identified? The earlier discussion of bankruptcy risk showed the importance of the share capital : assets ratio as well as the risk – return profile of the loan portfolio. The further assumption made in the present context is that loans made by the foreign offices of the banks have a higher risk–expected return profile at the margin so that a higher *fraction* of these loans in the balance sheet would imply higher bankruptcy risk for a given capital ratio. It is further possible, for the individual bank, that an increase in the *volume* of foreign lending would be associated with a rise in such risk. This would be the case if the effective degree of country diversification were to diminish, as could arise if the growth of loan demand were to issue from a subset of existing country borrowers. In the context of the present study such a source of rising risk is a realistic prospect since so much of the increased lending went to a limited number of oil-dependent NICs (cf. Chapter 1). It may be noted that with an increasing number of newly lending banks in this market, achieving initial diversification from international lending, there would be no need for market interest rates to reflect the growing weight of country risk in the portfolios of the 'mature' bank lenders with which we are concerned in this study. It will be argued below that the 'sequential' entry of newly diversifying banks into the market imposed added adjustment requirements on earlier lenders.

In addition to these risk-based sources of increasing cost from foreign lending, rising real resource costs will also be involved in maintaining an enlarged volume of overseas loan and deposit business. The use of real resource inputs by banking intermediaries has been emphasized by Sealey and Lindley (1977), although in the present context rising capital and labour costs would appear particularly likely for the domestic loan and deposit business of the banks. Reference has been made to the major legal impediments which the leading American banks have had to circumvent in expanding their domestic loan and deposit business. Foreign lending in contrast has been able to take advantage fully in developments in information technology much moderating rising unit costs on this score.

The formal model set out in Appendix B, therefore, assumes maximization of expected profits on the basis of market-determined interest rates for deposits and loans. Real resource costs, however, rise with an increase in *size* and with an increase in the *share* of domestic, as opposed to foreign, deposits and loans. Risk-related costs, on the other hand, rise with assets and with the share of foreign loans in the balance sheet.

What are the implications, in a model of bank behaviour formulated in this way, of a relative change in the cost of foreign deposits and on the return on overseas loans? What will govern the extent to which a reduction in the former, and an increase in the latter, causes the ratio of each to rise in the balance sheet?

Considering such influences separately, a fall in the relative cost of foreign deposits would be the result of the growth of OPEC revenues in the mid 1970s. The comparative static properties of the model are consistent with the intuitive position that balance sheet size would increase, with both equity capital and domestic deposits (as alternative sources of funds) experiencing a relative decline in their share of funding. This would, of course, be reinforced to the extent that equity was to remain a relatively expensive source of finance despite its ability to offset some of the risks of increased balance sheet size. Without more detailed specification of the two cost functions involved a definite answer as to the way each ratio will move is not possible. However, it is clear that this outcome will be crucially affected by the marginal impact of share capital on the potential insolvency cost function, and of the domestic deposit ratio on the resource cost function as domestic loans and balance sheet size change in each case. As formulated the model stresses that management must weigh marginal real resource costs of a change in domestic deposits and loans against the increased potential risk (and cost) of emergency adjustments in the face of threatened insolvency when size and foreign lending rise.

Given real resource costs the model also notes the potential link between a change in the domestic deposit ratio (down in the present context) and a change in the domestic loan ratio. The latter would tend to move in the opposite direction as resources were reallocated. High marginal resource costs of increasing the share of domestic loans in the balance sheet as size increased would then need to be invoked in explaining why the ratio did not rise in fact between the opening and closing dates.

Turning now to a rise in the perceived rate of return on foreign lending (relative to other business), the share of domestic loans would be expected to fall in an expanded overall balance sheet. Again, this fall in the relative size of domestic loan business could lead to a rise in the domestic deposit ratio unless the marginal resource costs relative to those of an increase in size were high. To the extent, of course, that the maintenance of a certain level of domestic deposits was much separated from the 'production' of domestic loans, the connection may in any case be weak (cf. Sealey and Lindley, 1977).

In these adjustments, then, three features are suggested as being compatible with the balance sheet changes witnessed between the beginning and end of the period of study. First, share capital apparently remained expensive relative to the deposit funds, notwithstanding its potentially beneficial effect in reducing overall bank risk as the size of the balance sheet increased. Secondly, the developments observed would be compatible with rising marginal resource costs inhibiting the share of domestic loan and deposit business, again as scale increased. Finally, in so far as the model captures the major constraints acting on management, the 'trade-off' between *real* resource costs, particularly in the development of domestic business, and the *potential* costs associated with avoiding insolvency, as riskier loans expand is made clear.

It would be natural to reverse this reasoning to explain the apparent adjustments after 1977. Thus the widely remarked reduction in 'spreads' on foreign lending in the later 1970s would be consistent with decreased emphasis on such lending, some revival in domestic business and an improvement in the share capital contribution as actually witnessed (Economist, 1984). The latter would largely result from a curtailment of asset size in the present static model. Interpreting these results in terms of growing nominal magnitudes, a fall in expected returns to foreign lending would require a *downward* adjustment of costs in the face of *increased* relative concentration on domestic loans. With share capital expensive, relative to the benefits it is thought to bring, the more the adjustment would need to be in terms of a slowed expansion of the balance sheet.

Effectively this adjustment implies that the banks would restrain the growth of their own share of expanding loan business, and this appears to have been the case in practice. The argument that the growth of foreign lending is determined by the growth of share capital is frequently made by bankers as a statement of internal policy and is now supported by regulation. Since shareholders' capital is usually augmented by retained profits, diminishing spreads on foreign loans exert further downward pressure on the growth of this business. However, an important consideration arises at this stage concerning the nature of the costs to which managements were responding in reducing their share of available loan activity. To the extent that the marginal costs of maintaining loans and deposits at the current level were actually being incurred, as for example in resource costs, *or if depositors were actually demanding a risk premium,* there would be good reason to expect full adjustment to the new market parameters. However, it appears to be the case in practice that the real resource costs of foreign-based lending and deposit taking were, at the margin, rather low. Presumably, therefore, the major cost consideration for management must relate to the evaluation of risk and the *potential* costs of emergency adjustment. Accordingly the decision of the bank to curtail its loan activity depends in part on the conviction with which those assessments are made. Until actually incurred, these are *notional* costs to set against the real current resource costs of expanding domestic lending activity. The previous chapter traced the difficulties and imprecision of country risk assessment and our consideration of bank adjustment patterns now suggests that, faced with the need to curtail currently profitable business, risk assessments previously made may well come under pressure for adjustment.

This line of reasoning appears to be broadly consistent with the institutional discussion in the previous chapter and it is also interesting in this connection that the major American banks were increasingly making representations for 'fair' access to domestic loan and deposit markets as the decade drew to a close. In terms of our discussion, a wider domestic loan portfolio would significantly reduce the need to curtail the growth of overall bank business. Similarly the increasing emphasis on liability management and the growing use of relatively cheap short term funds, which, we have noted, would help to compensate downward pressure on lending margins.

It is of interest, finally, to reconcile this downward pressure on international loan spreads, which certainly occurred, with the costly adjustment process just outlined. The proximate cause of the downward pressure on spreads was a continuing growth in supply, increasingly dominated by banks newly diversifying into the international arena. The regional American banks are an important example of 'new entrants' gaining, evidently, relatively profitable loan diversification for portfolios previously dominated by domestic American business. These new competitors, attracted by the previously high profits of sovereign lending, enjoyed lower 'costs' than the established lenders at their stage of diversification, and, for them, there was nothing necessarily reckless about the expansion. However, by initiating a downward trend in spreads they may well have obliged the more established banks to accept a heavier relative commitment to foreign lending than they would previously have been willing to contemplate had they known that returns would decline.

This reasoning underlines a crucial distinction between competitive behaviour in conventional industries and that which applies in banking. In the latter 'new entrants' may well enjoy lower 'costs' simply because they have differing initial portfolio positions and not because they are more efficient in any real sense. None the less the downward pressure on the product price continues and may leave some institutions with a higher level of risk than they would previously have wanted to bear.

A further distinguishing feature of banking competition, of course, is that competitive 'success' which threatens to damage a major competitor may have serious consequences for the other firms in the event of a crisis of confidence. This paradox is particularly relevant, of course, in the context of the discussion in Chapter 4, where the interconnection between banks was emphasized.

It has to be stressed that this interpretation of events is highly tentative and follows from the assumptions of a static model of bank balance sheet adjustment. All that can be claimed is that it is a plausible interpretation of the balance sheet data, and that it also appears compatible with impressionistic evidence, including that gained in conversation with practising bankers. If it should be the case that the thesis is broadly correct, the conclusion drawn from it, and from the discussion in Chapter 5, would be that a *fundamentally* unstable system has evolved in meeting the demand for international intermediation. The instability is at least in part due to the official initiatives which have appeared to protect depositors from risk of loss. The narrative of this chapter suggests that management, in a competitive environment, may be inappropriately placed to judge the risks involved. The discussion in Chapter 5, however, indicated the genuine difficulty of deciding what the risks actually were and the question arises as to whether depositors would be better able to judge if circumstances had called upon them to do so. A proper judgement on these risks, according to our case studies in Chapter 3, would have required an ability to predict the major global economic dislocations of the early 1980s as well as the policy responses of the debtor nations.

In so far as the global economy benefitted from the recycling achieved by the banks in the 1970s, and if it would gain by avoiding prolonged recession in the debtor states, there would seem to be a case for multinational involvement to absorb some of the risk of sustained financial flows in the 1980s. The final chapter considers some possible, and arguably realistic, policy options in the light of the analysis presented here.

NOTES

1   A clear derivation of a formula establishing the relationship between a firm's market value and its systematic risk is provided by Mossin (1969). This formula also reveals that if a firm's returns co-vary in a sufficiently negative manner with the variance of other returns, the market value of these shares may have a premium attached.
2   For instance the Federal Reserve Board issued a press notice on 8 November 1978, outlining new procedures for assessing country risk and the Comptroller of the Currency in the US argued that loans to sovereign governments and their 'instrumentalities' should be regarded as one by the bank. Taken together, these should not exceed 10 per cent of bank capital.
3   The first bank's coefficient, however, estimated over a somewhat longer time span, is significant at more than the 20 per cent level.

APPENDIX A: SPECIFYING THE PROBABILITY OF BANK INSOLVENCY

The requirement is to specify the probability of occurrence of the critical level of loss. A result allowing us to do this is Chebyshev's inequality, which states that a random variable with a given mean (average) outcome has a probability of differing from the mean by an arbitrary amount as follows:

$$\Pr\left(|x-\bar{x}| \geqslant d\right) \leqslant \frac{\sigma^2}{d^2}.$$

Here, x is the variable and the expression states that the probability of its differing from its own mean by an absolute (positive or negative) arbitrary value, d, is less than or equal to the variance of x divided by d^2. To make use of this result in the present context we define x to be the *net* expected returns on the bank's entire asset portfolio. The critical level of losses given the bank's capital will be defined in terms of the mean expected return and the standard deviation of return as follows:

$$L = \bar{x} - k\sigma$$

(*NB:* L represents negative profits).

Here the critical (bankruptcy) level of losses occurs when net returns fall short of the mean by some multiple (k) of the standard deviation of returns. Interpreting the inequality in this way (Blair and Heggested, 1978),

$$\Pr\left(|x-\bar{x}| \geqslant \bar{x}-L\right) \leqslant \frac{\sigma^2}{(\bar{x}-L)^2}.$$

The absolute value notation within the brackets states that

$$-\bar{x} + L \geqslant x - \bar{x} \geqslant \bar{x} - L.$$

If we neglect the probability that the deviation will be a positive one (the right hand inequality) our left hand inequality relates to critical losses:[1]

$$\Pr\left(x \leqslant L\right) \leqslant \frac{\sigma^2}{(\bar{x}-L)^2}.$$

This final expression allows us to superimpose our ray on the diagram in the text since the probability is a ratio of the variance; (the square of the standard deviaton), at, say D and the (squared) vertical distance to D from L.

---

[1] This implies that our final measure overstates the probability of bankruptcy through neglecting the positive outcome (Shapiro, 1982, p. 732).

APPENDIX B: A MODEL OF BANK BALANCE SHEET ADJUSTMENT

The model derives from one suggested by Baltensperger (1980), with management able to decide on overall size and certain balance sheet ratios in the pursuit of maximum profitability:

$$R + L_D + L_F = K + D_D + D_F = A$$

or, in words, reserves (R) plus domestic and foreign loans (L_D, L_F) equal shareholders' equity (K) and domestic and foreign-based deposits (D_D, D_F) at any balance sheet scale (A).

The profit function to be maximized is

$$\pi = i_1 R + i_2 L_D + i_3 L_F - \rho K - r D_D - r_2 D_F - C$$
$$\left(\frac{L_D}{A}, \frac{D_D}{A}, A\right) - S\left(\frac{L_F}{A}, \frac{K}{A}, A\right)$$

Lower case letters refer to (market-determined) expected returns and costs of funding (ρ for the cost of equity).

The real resource cost function $(C(\cdot))$ displays rising costs which rise more severely in the face of domestic loan and deposit business increasing its share of the balance sheet for reasons discussed in the text. Similarly the (notional) cost function, arising through the possible occurrence of insolvency, may be assumed to rise with the degree of capital inadequacy (cf. Baltensperger, 1980). It is here assumed to rise with the proportion of foreign loans and with the size of the bank, but to be decreasing for K/A. The first arises from the assumption that a rising share of foreign loans, other things being equal, raises risk. Increased asset size, holding the ratios of L_F and K/A constant, is assumed to raise risk since foreign lending will be increasing in *volume* thus possibly increasing the level of country risk as country concentration in the loan portfolio increases. Capital inadequacy is clearly less likely at higher values of K/A.

Certain balance sheet ratios, as well as overall size, are decision variables for management. Expressing the balance sheet in ratio form:

$$\frac{R}{A} + \frac{L_D}{A} + \frac{L_F}{A} = \frac{K}{A} + \frac{D_D}{A} + \frac{D_F}{A}.$$

or

$$\alpha + \beta + (1 - \alpha - \beta) = \eta + \theta + (1 - \eta - \theta).$$

In this model two ratios could be chosen independently on either side of the balance sheet. To simplify, however, the (unrealistic) assumption is made that management maintains a common ratio of reserves to deposits irrespective of whether the deposits are domestic or foreign-based. Since, therefore,

$$(1-\eta)A = D_D + D_F,$$

a constant reserves to deposits ratio of $\bar{z}$ would imply that

$$R = \bar{z}(1-\eta)A \quad \text{or} \quad \bar{z}(1-\eta) = \alpha.$$

The profit function may now be rewritten in terms of the decision variables β, η, θ, A:

$$\pi = i_1 \bar{z}(1-\eta)A + i_2\beta A + i_3(1-\bar{z}(1-\eta)-\beta)$$
$$A - \rho\eta A - r_1\theta A - r_2(1-\eta-\theta)A - C(\beta,\theta,A) - S(\beta,\eta,A)$$

First order conditions for profit maximization are:

$$(i_2-i_3)A - C'_\beta - S'_\beta \qquad\qquad = 0, \tag{1}$$
$$(i_3-i_1)\bar{z}A - (\rho-r_2)A - S'_\eta \qquad = 0, \tag{2}$$
$$(r_2-r_1)A - C'_\theta \qquad\qquad\qquad = 0, \tag{3}$$
$$i_1\bar{z}(1-\eta) + i_2\beta + i_3(1-\bar{z}(1-\eta)-\beta) \tag{4}$$
$$-\rho\eta - r_1\theta - r_2(1-\eta-\theta) - C'_A - S'_A = 0,$$

where c'_A reflects the marginal resource cost of an increase in asset size. The other partial derivatives, indicated by primes, may be interpreted similarly in terms of their subscripts.

The intuitive meaning of the first order conditions is that (1), the interest differential between domestic and foreign loans, would reflect the balance between the rising resource cost of a change in the ratio of domestic loans to total assets (β) and the (diminished) notional costs of such a change associated with the possibility of insolvency.

A similar interpretation may be given to (2) where the premium of share capital costs over the cost of (foreign) deposits (after allowing for the opportunity cost of increased required reserves) is balanced by the marginal offset provided by an improved capital ratio to the potential costs of threatened insolvency.

In (3) the marginal resource cost of an increase in the ratio of domestic deposits to total assets (θ) must account for the higher interest cost of foreign *vis-à-vis* domestic deposits.

Finally (4) indicates that asset size (with asset and liabilities ratios determined) would be expanded to the point where weighted marginal cost was equal to weighted marginal revenue.

It is comparative static properties of this model with respect to changes in i_3 and r_2 which are reflected in the statements in the text.

7 Conclusion: Some possible policy options

If the phenomenon of a financial cycle applies at the international level, as it appears to do in the course of national economic cycles, 1982 would be seen as the termination point of the remarkable growth of international bank lending which was such a distinctive feature of the 1970s (cf. Ch. 2).

The major institutional features of this lending which we have discussed, syndicated loans and the supporting inter-bank market, experienced significant reverses associated with country debt difficulties. During that year 'spontaneous' syndicated loans fell in value below loans associated with the restructuring of country debt. The magnitude of the country debts involved in this restructuring reached $30 billion in 1982 and $60 billion in 1983. Roughly a quarter of the last figure involved new money, with twenty-two countries involved, and this alone was a significant discouragement to new lending unassociated with national debt renegotiations (Bank of England, 1984a). It is also noteworthy that, in 1982, international bond issues rose and syndicated credits fell so that rough parity was reached in the two forms of financing. Bond issues actually overtook syndicated credits in 1983, beginning what appeared to be a trend in favour of more 'marketable' debt (Montagnon, 1984a).

At the same time, country debt crises were having a profound effect on the inter-bank market. In most cases, maturities on rescheduled loans were extended for periods ranging from seven to nine years. While much of the obligations involved had been maturing long term debt, significant volumes of short term (less than twelve months) financial and trade credits were also included (BIS, 1984, p. 108). The effect of these procedures has been to 'lock in' banks for much longer periods to certain loans. As many such loans had been made through the inter-bank market, with commercial banks in borrower nations drawing on funds, smaller and regional banks began to withdraw inter-bank credit 'lines'. Doubts about the liquidity of the inter-bank market, which were examined in Chapter 4, were thus manifested in a tightening of conditions as these withdrawals occurred (Mendelsohn, 1983). In this connection the rescheduling of Brazilian and Mexican debts involved a commitment by banks to re-establish inter-bank lines.

These dislocations in what had been the most dynamic areas of growth in world capital markets in the 1970s were clearly related to events in the rest of the world economy in more than one way. The analysis of the growth of international bank lending in Chapter 4 made clear that, as a credit-rather than a money-creating phenomenon, its growth must bear some relationship to monetary conditions in national economies. A rise in the global money supply will tend to promote credit growth and vice versa. One example would be the increased lending by banks in 1977-8 when the OPEC surplus had temporarily disappeared. Funds were readily forthcoming from the USA where monetary policy was relaxed (BIS, 1983, p. 120).

For the major OECD economies, the years to 1979 had been years of mounting inflationary (and stagflationary) difficulties, whereas the period following was characterized by restrictive monetary conditions with reduction of the rate of inflation as the overriding target. With the increasing inflationary bias of these advanced economies, notably through expectations, the short run effects of concerted disinflation, in conjunction with the second round of oil price increases, were unpredictable (BIS, 1983, p. 10).

In retrospect, the effect was to produce an unexpectedly severe and prolonged global recession, the consequences of which included the financial difficulties of Brazil and Chile examined in Chapter 3. The increased restrictiveness of US monetary policy was supported by a change in the techniques of its operation in 1979 with dramatic consequences for global interest rates and the strength of the dollar. At the same time, the deteriorating trade conditions that we noted for the two countries mentioned applied generally after 1980. Export earnings from non-OPEC LDCs declined by 9 per cent in 1982, after an appreciable slow down in 1981 (BIS, 1983, p. 123).

The first signs of bank unease were visible in the latter half of 1979 when undisbursed credit commitments, relative to outstanding loans, began to decline appreciably, as they did through to the 1982 crisis. Recourse to short term financing steadily increased with the nervousness of the lenders. Events which conduced to this nervousness included the total rescheduling of Poland's debt in 1980 and the Falklands crisis of 1982. The latter appeared to act as a catalyst in heightening concern over the position of the major Latin American republics. Arguably the most important ingredient, however, was the Mexican crisis in 1982. That crisis, and the Brazilian one of late 1982 which it partially caused, ushered in a new era of officially sponsored rescheduling which some have seen as tantamount to a 'cartelization' of the international banking system (Dale, 1983).

In these major cases the IMF made complimentary bank financing a condition of assistance through the Fund's extended facility. Precedents for this existed from the 1980 case of Togo and that of

Sudan in 1981 (Mendelsohn, 1983). Contributions from the banks were based on quota allocations related to their existing country exposure (Bank of England, 1984b, p. 55).

By 1983, and particularly following the coming into force of the Eighth General Review of IMF quotas at the end of that year, it was evident that IMF financing was accounting for much of the growth in lending. Disbursements, net of repayments in previous drawings, appeared to be running at an average rate of $7 billion in 1983–4 compared with $1 billion in 1981–2 (Johnson, 1984). Thus, the two-pronged aspect of Fund financing, large scale credits, and the maintenance of adequate external (bank) funding, through making its own credits conditional on such provision, were the dominating feature of the proliferating rescheduling agreements of 1982–3. During the course of such negotiations, bridging loans have been provided by OECD central banks through the auspices of the BIS. The real implications of the Fund-led support programmes, for reasons made clear in the case study of Brazil, have been severe. As the BIS put it

> The heart of the international debt problem is in Latin America, where the balance of payments adjustment process entailed overall cuts in imports of nearly 50 per cent between 1981 and 1983. [BIS, 1984, p. 112.]

In somewhat more than a decade, then, the picture has changed from rapidly expanding international sovereign loan commitment by private banks to officially orchestrated measures to prevent a reversal in the face of substantial rescheduling needs. How might these events be interpreted and what criteria may be suggested for guiding policy reform? Seeking interpretation, as at the beginning of this enquiry, it is necessary to give some prominence to the oil price increases. Particular consequences of these events need to be singled out and the implications traced by reference to the analysis in earlier chapters.

It is, naturally, difficult to disentangle the effects of the price increases from other changes taking place in the world economy of the 1970s. Chapter 2 considered the investment shifts' argument which emphasized the gradual deterioration of investment opportunities in the industrialized nations in contrast with certain LDCs (the NICs), which had begun to follow 'outward looking' and apparently successful development strategies which welcomed foreign investment. This tendency alone may well have justified an enhanced flow of financial capital between countries as direct investment flows appear to confirm. However, the investment shifts argument implied an adjustment to gradually emerging incentives which would ramify over a number of years. On top of the 'structural' current account deficits which would be implied by capital inflow, the oil price increases superimposed a major new demand for balance of payments support. Expectations of rapid income growth were the 'collateral' for borrowing to ameliorate adjustment to the current loss of real income.

A retrospective position now shows that the oil crisis itself, and especially its global aftermath, had serious effects in terms of the constraints imposed on the economic performance of the borrower. What would normally have been a sound basis for borrowing was rendered less so by the events which had made it necessary. Most importantly, for lenders making decisions in the 1970s, the fundamental shifts of policy towards disinflation in the industrialized world after 1979 may not have been easily predicted. Much less so would have been the severity of the recession which followed or the associated behaviour of real interest rates and the value of the dollar. In terms of our discussion of risk in Chapters 5 and 6 the *systematic* risk of bank portfolios was due to rise in an unpredictable manner (Dale, 1983). Prior to the emergence of the 1982 difficulties analyses strongly suggested that adequate diversification of risk could be achieved even with a loan portfolio comprising a few countries (Eaton and Gersovitz, 1980). Evidence was available to show that previous debt service difficulties were essentially random and uncorrelated phenomena. This appeared even to be the case *within* Latin America, and bank loan portfolios which were heavily committed to that continent could therefore be seen as sound. Recent experience is clearly at variance with this point of view.

Possibly systematic risk was also rising for another reason associated with the oil price effects. Slack loan demand in the OECD nations certainly heightened the interest of lenders in the continuing borrowing needs of LDCs. This effect was drawn attention to by Sachs (1981) in the form of explaining the emergence of low real interest rates in the post 1973 period. A borrowers' market certainly emerged in the later 1970s, suggesting that banks' lending to LDCs was substituting, in part, for business they would normally have conducted in the industrialized countries. This business itself, of course, has been subject to systematic negative influences in recent years, which accounts for the failure of some banks, most notably of Continental Illinois.

From the point of view of lenders facing individual country borrowers then, contrary to the theoretical discussion in Chapter 5, the default probability schedule turned out not to be at all well defined (if rescheduling is regarded as default on the original loan terms). The apparent failure of country risk models within the banks left little resistance to the emergence of ambitious lending strategies based on the belief that sovereign lending was safer than domestic business.

As the credit rationing discussion emphasized, price setting in credit markets is open to particular difficulties given the adverse selection implications of higher interest rates to compensate for higher risk. Without relevant experience on default behaviour, difficulties of achieving a rational outcome multiply. In such circumstances the competitive process itself becomes destabilizing. In contrast with industrial or retail concerns, where success in competition depends on relative production efficiency, and product specification, banking competition comes to depend on the lowest risk perceptions, and hence the lowest loan rate setting. In this way the compression of 'spreads' witnessed between 1977 and 1980 would be indicative. Hindsight suggests that country risk takes time to build up so that penalties for excessive risk taking are not immediately apparent. Much the same argument can be applied to the enormous influx of new banks to the business during the same period. Whereas cautious bankers may have wanted to ration credit to individual national borrowers, more aggressive new lenders could offer further funds, cutting away the basis of calculation for earlier loan contracts. Arguably, the market was unable to arrive at a credit-rationed equilibrium in the circumstances prevailing at the time (cf. the concluding section of Ch. 6).

The upshot of this for borrowers was that real interest rates on international loans were low. Two reasons have been mentioned: the increased availability of funds following the oil price increases together with reduced credit demand in the recession hit industrialized countries, and the process of intermediation itself. Unfortunately, as we have seen, policy shifts in these major economies have changed the circumstances in a substantially adverse manner.

In summary, then, the systematic risk of investments was increased in the aftermath of the oil crisis. Paradoxically, however, the increased savings initially accrued to oil-exporting governments who displayed a pronounced risk aversion in their choice of savings instruments. Their choice of wholesale bank deposits despite their low, and even negative, real rates of return reflected this position.

For financial intermediaries satisfactorily to reconcile the riskiness of borrowers with the security needs of savers, the logic of our theoretical discussion in Chapter 6 was that more risk capital would be needed. As our examples showed, however, the opposite was the case, with equity capital declining as a fraction of total assets. In the face of strong competition, and a sanguine view of risk, capital issues were an expensive form of funding. Since apparently satisfactory diversification could be achieved through participation in loan syndications, capital could be economized. It may be noted here that the model in Chapter 6 implies heavier gearing (a higher deposits to equity ratio) if bank management were seeking to maximize the return on shareholders' equity. This was certainly a priority until the late 1970s when the return on total assets (RCTA) became an additional major objective. If depositors do not demand risk premia, and this again appears to have been the case, pressures for increased gearing are even more apparent. In the eyes of some commentators, the failure of deposit rates to forestall 'excessive' risky lending is the crux of the issue and, as suggested in Chapter 6, may have thrown an inappropriate risk assessment function on to management alone.

For the present the favourable terms on which deposits were available certainly were a force for expansion, and their use in the form of lucrative loans could be facilitated by the technique of syndication. The merit of this process was that the capital of more banks could be involved in a single loan increasing the margin of safety for each institution. The smaller banks were able to 'tap' the available deposits through the inter-bank market whereas other banks were attracted by the implicit information revealed by the participation in loans of the major banking names.

Thus, while syndication increased the bank capital backing of sovereign loans it has tended *itself* to increase the perceived risk of these loans when exogenous events cause major debt crisis as occurred in 1982. When difficulties mount, as was noted in Chapter 5, time horizons adopted by lending institutions become shorter, with the immediate cash flow position of the borrower becoming a key concern. Indeed, the present standing of the borrower, as revealed by recent terms achieved in the market, was noted as increasing its importance in the eyes of lenders.

In addition to the failure of models based on more substantial borrower-specific factors which were discussed in Chapter 5, there is a further logic in these myopic indicators deriving from the syndication process. For a country with many creditors, credit worthiness as far as the individual lender is concerned depends *not* on an objective view of each country's prospects but on how willing others will be to continue to provide funds. Looking over each others' shoulders, banks tend to reduce credit lines together, and this allegedly occurred during the summer of 1982 (Dale, 1983). The tendency for the system to unravel once confidence was shaken necessitated the forceful official interventions through the IMF and BIS which have been mentioned.

Recalling Fama's description of the probable evolution of an entirely unregulated banking system with various risk classes of deposits, an ability correctly to anticipate the level of bank lending risk which actually occurred would have been expected to lead to a greater emphasis on risk capital than we have observed. Moreover, if the threat of default originating from an exogenous rise in real interest rates, or decline in export earnings, had been gauged before the event, the market might have been expected to generate alternative types of debt instruments for borrowers allowing some flexibility in repayment schedules. Instead, banks relied heavily on deposits rather than risk-bearing funds and LDC borrowers took on syndicated loans which offered no (previously acknowledged) flexibility in repayment in the face of exogenously determined losses. Indeed, one of the specific advantages of financial intermediation, the spreading of risk (where the institution is able to absorb losses on part of a wide portfolio without threatening the wealth of savers) became impossible on the terms negotiated.

Again in retrospect, the borrowers' risks were magnified. Interest rate risk has already been noted to have been passed to the borrower by the use of floating rates based on LIBOR. Similarly, there has been observed a perverse relationship between debt service payments and terms of trade changes. The mechanism behind this would be that a country with substantial external debts would find its service payments magnifying the volatility of national income *available for national use*. Consequently even greater reliance on external finance is required to produce the same degree of smoothing which the borrowing was intended to produce. This fundamental problem with fixed terms funds is exacerbated if debt service payments themselves vary perversely with national income, as happened to occur in the early 1980s (Lessard, 1983). This confluence of events was noted in the case studies of Chapter 3. As Lessard points out, the only way in these circumstances for risk shifting to be achieved, to the benefit of a borrower suffering exogenous shocks, is for insistence on renegotiation of terms in the form of rescheduling. The fact that such an event was not allowed for in the original terms, however, contributes to a crisis of confidence in the institutions affected.

The inappropriateness of the form of financing which occurred has been argued to be the result of the underestimation of the risks which were to become manifest as the ramifications of the oil price increases unfolded. The impact of this on bank lending decisions has been discussed here and in Chapter 5. On the other hand, the relative quiescence of depositors has increasingly been put down to the implicit guarantees contained in the Basle type accords discussed in Chapter 6 (especially Swoboda, 1982). According to this argument, the belief that major banks were likely to be rescued by national government action meant that funds were available to such banks on favourable terms. Certainly the fundamental importance of ready access to capital markets implicit in the funding of the two banks in

Chapter 6 is consistent with this view. Not only large banks but large national borrowers may have been inadvertantly subsidized by the moral dilemma of official involvement. In this way, the risks of large banks are *actually* smaller than for other institutions. Large national borrowers also achieve a degree of leverage in the belief that they will not be allowed to get to the position where default arises. According to Swoboda, this is the crux of the problem. It may be noted that in these circumstances risk is effectively shifted, but, through IMF involvement it is shifted to national tax payers. Thus, to the extent that the banks have evolved in such a way that risk-bearing funds are inadequate to cover the potential losses, either depositors or the wider public will unintentionally become involved.

In assessing possible policy initiatives, so many have been proposed that immediate practicability and consistency with the present position would be a convenient criterion to adopt. Secondly, as perception of risk has taken the central place in this analysis, a further criterion might be that any proposal should contribute to allowing some risks arising from exogenous sources, for example interest rate shocks, to be passed on to the financial institutions involved or to the international community at large (Lessard, 1983). For this not to lead to further difficulties the banks themselves would need to be more satisfactorily funded.

In terms of compatibility with present circumstances, the much less sanguine view of sovereign debt now prevailing within the banks, and amongst depositors, would be expected to lead, through market mechanisms, to relevant adjustments even ignoring official intervention. Our model in Chapter 6 suggested that a bank with a high fraction of (relatively risky) foreign to total loans would be less likely to increase the weight in its portfolio of loans in that direction, given an improvement in expected returns, than would a bank less heavily involved. The evidence of Chapter 6 was that two major institutions had initiated adjustment at the approach of the 1980s, and the most recently available BIS Annual Report (BIS, 1984) suggests strongly that such adjustments have been occurring on a general level. Thus it is reported that exposure to LDCs was growing less quickly than profit retentions, which may be seen as equity funding. Moreover, there has been a distinct shift away from inter-bank funding and a corresponding increase in the reliance on floating rate notes. Again relevant to the Fama model, a substantial part of these issues, especially by American banks, was equity linked or in the form of subordinated debt. The volume of these notes rose from $8 billion in 1981 to $13 billion in 1982 and $14 billion in 1983 (BIS, 1984, p. 108).

Although adjustments of this type could well have arisen

spontaneously, official guidelines on capital adequacy have undoubtedly added to the pressure to increase risk capital.

Similar shifts away from syndicated credits to international bonds in the form of floating rate note issues have been occurring on the lending side. Despite lower returns to the lender there is a premium on marketability and the general escape of bonds from rescheduling crises also suggest greater security for the lender. These issues have been seen by some commentators as a necessary portfolio balance to offset high yielding, but high risk, rescheduled sovereign loans (Montagnon, 1984). The latter do remain high yielding given the substantial spreads on rescheduled debt, frequently in excess of 2 per cent and fees of over 1 per cent have also been imposed (BIS, 1984, p. 108).

A further trend in the direction of strengthening balance sheet positions may be noted since it involves a reversal of another unintended incentive to overseas lending. This is the tendency to domestic deregulation in a number of major industrial countries. Perhaps most notably, the adoption of the Depository Institutions Deregulation and Monetary Control Act and the establishment of International Banking Facilities in the United States occurred in 1980. This has enhanced the ability of the major banks to compete on a wider front for domestic business, affording further opportunities for balance sheet diversification (cf. the discussion in Chapter 6).

On this interpretation of events, the problem is probably not so much the safety of the banks as the continued willingness to supply funds to LDCs in the wake of the reassessment which has taken place. Bank balance sheets are in the process of being strengthened but without official involvement this would be very much at the expense of such flows.

The new IMF–BIS approach has already been noted and despite its cartel-like characteristics, continuing involvement may be the only way in future of avoiding the credit market instability analysed in earlier chapters. The continuing need for IMF involvement, consistent with what was said there, stems from the requirement for a 'cap' on total indebtedness. In this connection the institution acts to substitute for a number of non-price mechanisms which exist to make domestic loan markets more stable than they would otherwise be. These range from *conventions* seriously acknowledged by borrowers and lenders, for instance the 'quick assets ratio' applied to industrial firms, to *legal* measures. Bond covenants are available which restrict the borrower from carrying out certain actions *after* a debt has been incurred which would endanger the security of the lender. These may include overall debt ceilings, (Lomax, 1983; Dale, 1983). IMF guidelines and monitoring of national borrowers could provide a similar function. With continued involvement by official agencies, however, moral hazard again becomes potentially serious. Overlending by banks would be likely in the belief that that involvement reduced country risks. Consequently, a number of proposals have been put forward linking bank lending to explicit IMF approval (Lever, 1983; Laulan, 1983). Effectively these proposals amount to loan guarantee schemes where new bank lending is covered in the same way as much export trade, probably by national agencies, as in the Lever plan. The essential role for continuing IMF presence is obvious given the otherwise increased incentive for overlending (Dorrance, 1981). The insurance provision is the incentive for bank co-operation in notifying the Fund of intended loans and for seeking prior Fund approval. Again, detailed IMF supervision would probably be necessary to prevent insurance premiums themselves becoming an onerous burden on the ultimate borrower either directly or through increased charges from the banks. If Fund activity reduced these premiums the need for some restraint in the form of suveillance of economic policies would be an essential additional restraint.

Loan guarantee schemes under IMF auspices are intended to support continued lending to LDCs when the circumstances might indicate a substantial contraction for reasons already discussed. Present involvement, though not explicitly incorporating loan guarantees, has succeeded in preventing a more severe contraction in credit facilities. In this respect something of a country 'lender of last resort' function has emerged with finance from the Fund assisting countries with their (rescheduled) debt servicing. In the same way that domestic central banks provide this facility for commercial banks suffering a deposit outflow (albeit at penalty interest rates), Fund/BIS finance, involving conditionality, has a parallel function in sustaining bank confidence after crisis events. The need for conditionality, however, again must be stressed given the incentive for governments to over borrow, and for banks to overlend, when country risk factors become a less pressing consideration.

The role of multilateral institutions in preventing major borrowers from being declared in default has direct implications not only for continuing funding of these borrowers but also as a means of preventing bank failure. This, indeed, has been one of the most important reasons for its emergence and has a number of domestic parallels (Grubel, 1979). Existing loans remain on bank balance sheets as performing assets and solvency is maintained. Once more to emphasize the point, such a system can only be sensibly sustained if it is not permitted to lead to unwise expansion of loans depriving potentially superior uses of necessary funds.

While lender of last resort facilities for sovereign borrowers protect the solvency of banks heavily involved, other suggested schemes have aimed particularly at the illiquidity threat to banks as crises of confidence cause bulk deposit withdrawals, and a seizure of the inter-bank market, the possibility of which was examined in Chapter 4. The most obvious approach to this problem would be that envisaged in existing international understandings. Lender of last resort facilities would be provided by central banks of the relevant countries to the head offices of the banks concerned. These would then channel the funds to their international offices which may be experiencing difficulties, perhaps as a result of credit rationing in the inter-bank market.

Although this must be an essential emergency weapon, given the interrelations discussed in Chapter 4, it suffers the disadvantage that it may help to sustain in business some banks for whom the initiating deposit withdrawal was a rational response to poor management and excessively risky banking practices. This would arise because lender of last resort facilities must be automatic, not discretionary, to sustain confidence in them (Dean and Giddy, 1981a).

One frequently discussed approach to forestalling crises of confidence in the banks but which would not at the same time give protection to incompetently managed organizations, is to extend national deposit insurance schemes to the international deposits of those nations' banks. This procedure has already been adopted for German banks since 1976, when Deutschemark-denominated deposits at the local branches of foreign banks became insured (Grubel, 1979, p. 12). While Grubel's influential proposal was for an international deposit insurance corporation, this would imply a very substantial organization with considerable powers to investigate the banks covered. It is questionable whether such an approach is currently feasible (Dean and Giddy, 1981a). The last-mentioned authors propose a more modest scheme financed by central banks for their own banks' international liabilities. An insurance premium would be based on the assessed riskiness of each bank's international portfolio – not to raise revenues for the fund but to discourage imprudence. Banks would be free to choose their portfolios given that the variable 'tax' will be involved.

A distinguishing feature of this scheme is that not all international deposits would be covered. Limits could be placed on deposit size or possibly according to 'senior' or 'junior' claim on liquidated assets. Depositors would then be given a choice of risk/return combination and the details of which deposits were covered would be made public. In this way a helpful move in the direction of raising a risk capital element of bank funding would be achieved, substantially lessening the fears of general deposit withdrawal (Dean and Giddy, 1981b).

These measures, which are already either operative or fairly readily arranged at the national level, suggest that a collapse of the major lending banks can probably be avoided given quick action to forestall a total default by a large sovereign borrower.

As noted earlier, however, the fundamental problem must continue to be an adequate flow of financial resources to sustain economic growth in the developing countries. The existing burden of indebtedness for some of these nations, as our two case studies indicated, will continue to drag in the opposite direction. Those studies implied that part of the difficulty had arisen through the inability of the borrower nations to shift the risk of 'exogenous' shocks, for example, rising interest rates, to the intermediaries on a contractual basis. Accordingly, and on a somewhat more innovative note, attention might be given in future rescheduling negotiations to the contractual fixing of the *real* rate of interest with the principal being readjusted periodically with respect to an international price index. Further contractual flexibility could be achieved by allowing the borrower to deviate, within pre-arranged limits, from equal installment debt repayment schedules. Thus, if export earnings were to decline, repayments could fall to be made up later. For new finance, project-specific risk capital might be a useful source of flexibility with the lender being guaranteed a share of the *output* of the project financed, as might bonds linked to the volume of world trade in particularly relevant commodities (Lessard, 1983).

Designing these instruments to be marketable would have appeal for the banks, although an increased proportion of risk capital in total funding would be necessary to accommodate a big increase in variable return loans. An official alternative, or complement, to these measures would be an expansion of the IMF compensatory financing facility to cover drawings made necessary by exogenously caused changes in the debt service burden.

All of these measures would assist a beneficial shifting of risk from the shoulders of borrower nations. Hopefully, these risks themselves will be reduced by a re-emergence of sustainable global economic expansion and trade during the remainder of the decade.

References

Akerlof, G. (1970) 'The market for lemons: qualitative uncertainty and the market mechanism', *Quarterly Journal of Economics,* Vol. 84, pp. 488–500.

Amex (1984) 'International debt; banks and the LDCs', *The Amex Bank Review Special Paper,* No. 10, March 1984.

Anderson, T. (1982) 'More models than *Vogue* magazine', *Euromoney,* November 1982, pp. 41–6.

Anderson, T. and Field, P. (1982) 'The tremors that threaten the banking system', *Euromoney,* October 1982, pp. 17–31.

Angelini, A., Eng, M. and Lees, F. A. (1979) *International Lending, Risk and the Euromarkets* (London: Macmillan).

Argy, V. (1981) *The Post War International Money Crisis: An Analysis* (Allen and Unwin).

Artis, M. J. and Lewis, J. K. (1981) *Monetary Control in the United Kingdom* (Oxford: Philip Allan).

Baer, W. (1972) 'Import substitution and industrialisation in Latin America: Experiences and interpretations', *Latin American Research Review,* Vol. 7, pp. 95–111.

Baltensperger E. (1980) 'Alternative approaches to the theory of the banking firm', *Journal of Monetary Economics,* Vol. 6, pp. 1–57.

Bank of England (1984a) 'International financial developments', *Bank of England Quarterly Bulletin,* Vol. 24, June 1984, pp. 180–8.

Bank of England (1984b) 'International banking markets in 1983', *Bank of England Quarterly Bulletin,* Vol. 24, March 1984, pp. 54–68.

Banker (1971) 'Commentary 2: Controlling the Eurodollar market', *The Banker,* July 1971, p. 749.

Beckhart, B. H. (1972) *Federal Reserve System* (Washington, D.C.: American Institute of Banking).

Berger F. E. (1981) 'The emerging transformation of the US banking system', *The Banker,* September 1981, pp. 25–39.

Bergsman, J. (1970) *Brazil: Industrialization and Trade Policies* (Oxford: OUP).

BIS (1983) *Bank for International Settlements: Fifty-third Annual Report* (Washington, D.C.: BIS).

BIS (1984) *Bank for International Settlements: Fifty-fourth Annual Report* (Washington D.C.: BIS).

Blair, R. D. and Heggestad, A. A. (1979) 'Bank portfolio regulation and the probability of bank failure', *Journal of Money, Credit and Banking,* Vol. 10, pp. 88–93.

Bond, T. D. and Briault, C. B. (1983) 'Commercial banks and international debt: A problem of control?', October 1983, Bank of England (mimeo).

Carron, A. S. (1982) 'Financial crises: Recent experience in U.S. and international markets', *Brookings Papers on Economic Activity*, Vol. 2, pp. 395–422.

Carvounis, C. (1982) 'The LDC debt problem: trends in country risk analysis and rescheduling exercises', *Columbia Journal of World Business*, Spring 1982, pp. 15–19.

Cline, W. R. (1984) *International Debt: Systemic Risk and Policy Response* (Cambridge, Mass.: MIT Press).

Cline, W. R. and Weintraub S. (1981) *Economic Stabilization in Developing Countries* (Washington, D.C.: Brookings Institution).

Dale, R. S. (1983) 'Country risk and bank regulation', *The Banker*, Vol. 133, March 1983, pp. 41–8.

Dean, J. W. and Giddy, I. H. (1981a) *Averting International Banking Crises*, Monograph Series in Finance and Economics No. 1 (New York: Graduate School of Business Administration, New York University).

Dean, J. W. and Giddy, I. H. (1981b) 'Six ways to world banking safety', *Euromoney*, May 1981b, pp. 128–35.

Diaz-Alejandro, C. F. (1983) 'Some aspects of the 1982–3 Brazilian payments crisis' *Brookings Papers on Economic Activity*, Vol. 10, pp. 701–8.

Dornbusch, R. (1982) 'Stabilization policies in developing countries: what have we learned?', *World Development*, Vol. 10, pp. 701–8.

Dornbusch, R. (1983) 'Comments on Diaz-Alejandro (1983)', *Brookings Papers on Economic Activity*, Vol. 2, pp. 547–3.

Dorrance, G. (1981) 'Would loan guarantees undermine international capital markets?', *The Banker*, Vol. 131, December 1981, pp. 39–41.

Eaton, J. and Gersovitz, M. (1980a) 'LDC participation in international financial markets: Debt and reserves', *Journal of Development Economics*, Vol. 7, pp. 3–21.

Eaton, J. and Gersovitz, M. (1980b) 'Poor country borrowing in private financial markets and the repudiation issue', Discussion Paper 94 (International Finance Section, Princeton University, Princeton, N.J.).

Eaton, J. and Gersovitz, M. (1981) 'Debt with potential repudiation: theoretical and empirical analysis', *Review of Economic Studies*, Vol. 48, pp. 289–309.

Economist (1982) 'A survey of international banking', *The Economist*, 20 March 1982.

Economist (1984) 'A survey of international banking', *The Economist* 24 March 1984.

Ellis, J. G. (1981) 'Eurobanks and the interbank market', *Bank of England Quarterly Bulletin*, Vol. 21, pp. 351–64.

Fama, E. F. (1980) 'Banking in the theory of finance', *Journal of Monetary Economics*, Vol. 6, pp. 39–57.

Feder, G. (1980) 'Economic growth, foreign loans and debt servicing capacity of developing countries', *Journal of Development Studies*, Vol. 16; pp. 352–69.

Financial Times (1984) Leading article, 24 May 1984.

Foxley, A. (1982) 'Towards a free market economy: Chile 1974–79', *Journal of Development Economics*, Vol. 10, pp. 3–29.

Galbraith E. (1971) [Speech extracts.] *The Banker*, 14 April 1971.

Goodman, L. S. (1980) 'The pricing of syndicated Eurocurrency credits', *Federal Reserve Bank of New York Quarterly Review*, Summer, 1980, pp. 39–49.

Goodman, L. S. (1981) 'Bank lending to non-OPEC LDCs: are risks diversifiable', *Federal Reserve Bank of New York Quarterly Review*, Summer 1981, pp. 10–12.

Grabbe, J. O. (1982) 'Liquidity creation and maturity transformation in the Eurodollar market', *Journal of Monetary Economics*, Vol. 10, pp. 39–72.

Grubel, H. G. (1979) 'A proposal for the establishment of an international deposit insurance corporation', Essays in International Finance No. 133, (Princeton, N.J.: International Finance Section, Department of Economics, Princeton University).

Gurley, J. G. and Shaw, E. S. (1960) *Money in a Theory of Finance* (Washington, D.C.: Brookings Institution).

Hardy, C. (1982) 'Rescheduling developing country debts 1956–1980; Lessons and recommendations', Overseas Development Council Working Paper No. 1 (Washington).

Hewson, J. (1975) *Liquidity Creation and Distribution in the Eurocurrency Markets* (Lexington, Mass.: Lexington Books).

Hewson, J. and Sakakibara, E. (1974) 'The Eurodollar deposit multiplier: a portfolio approach', *IMF Staff Papers*, Vol. 21, London: pp. 307–28.

Hogan, W. P. and Pierce, I. F. (1982) *The Incredible Eurodollar* (London: Allen and Unwin).

IBRD (1981) *World Development Report 1981* (New York: OUP).

IBRD (1981a) *World Debt Tables* (Washington, D.C.: IBRD).

IMF (1980) *World Economic Outlook 1980* (Washington, D.C.: IMF).

IMF (1981) *IMF World Economic Outlook 1981* (Washington, D.C.: IMF).

IMF (1984) *IMF World Economic Outlook 1984* (Washington, DC.: IMF).

Jaffee, D. M. and Russell, T. (1976) 'Imperfect information, uncertainty, and credit rationing', *Quarterly Journal of Economics*, Vol. 90, pp. 651–66.

Johnson, C. (1984) 'International bank lending after the slowdown', *The Banker*, Vol. 134, January 1984, pp. 23–6.

Johnson, H. G. (1958) 'The transfer problem and exchange stability' in his *International Trade and Economic Growth*, pp. 169–90. (London: Allen and Unwin).

Kaletsky, A. (1984) 'A dismal outlook-for some', *Financial Times*, 25 May, 1984, p. 22.

Kahn, M. S. and Knight M. D. (1983) 'Determinants of current account balances of non-oil developing countries in the 1970s: an empirical analysis', *IMF Staff Papers*, Vol. 30, pp. 819–43.

Kindleberger, C. P. (1978) 'Debt situation of the developing countries in historical perspective' in *Financing and Risk in Developing Countries*, edited by S. H. Goodman (New York: Praeger).

Kindleberger, C. P. (1981) 'Quantity and price, especially in financial markets' in *International Money: A Collection of Essays* (London: Allen and Unwin).

Laulan, Y. (1983) 'A new approach to international indebtedness', *The Banker*, Vol. 133, June 1983, pp. 25–9.

Lessard, D. (1983) 'North–south: the implications for multinational banking', *Journal of Banking and Finance*, Vol. 7, pp. 521–36.

Lever, H. (1983) 'The Lever plan', *The Economist*, 9 July 1983, pp. 19–20.

Lomax, D. (1983) 'Sovereign risk analysis now', *The Banker*, Vol. 133, January 1983, pp. 33–9.

McKinnon, R. I. (1980) 'Foreign exchange policy and economic liberalization in less developed countries', paper presented at the Conference on Financial Policy in Small Open Economies, Santiago, Chile, 21–22 January, 1980.

Mayer, H. W. (1976) 'The BIS concept of the Eurocurrency market', *Euromoney*, May 1976, pp. 60–6.

Mayne L. (1980) 'Bank dividend policy and holding company affiliation', *Journal of Financial and Quantitative Analysis*, Vol. 15, p. 469.

Mendelsohn, S. (1980) *Money on the Move: The Modern International Capital Market* (New York: McGraw-Hill).

Mendelsohn, M. S. (1983) 'International debt crisis: the practical lessons of restructuring', *The Banker*, Vol. 133, July 1983, pp. 33–8.

Minsky, H. P. (1982) 'Debt deflation process in today's institutional environment', *Banca Nazionale del Lavoro*, Vol. 35, pp. 375–93.

Montagnon, P. (1983) 'A jolt to be remembered', *Financial Times*, 1 March 1983, p. 18.

Montagnon, P. (1984a) 'Profound changes in structure', in a survey of international capital markets, *Financial Times*, 19 March 1984, p. 1.

Montagnon, P. (1984b) 'Mexico's pace-setting way forward', *Financial Times*, 12 September 1984, p. 25.

Mossin, J. (1969) 'Security pricing and investment criteria in competitive markets', *American Economic Review*, Vol. 59, p. 749.

Newlyn, W. T. (1977) *The Financing of Economic Development* (Oxford: OUP).

OECD (1981) *Development Co-operation 1981 Review* (Paris: OECD).

OECD (1983) *Development Co-operation 1983 Review* (Paris: OECD).

Pringle R. (1966) 'Why US banks go overseas', *The Banker*, November 1966, p. 77.

Reid, M. (1982) *The Secondary Banking Crisis 1973–75: Its Causes and Course* (London: Macmillan).

Saade, N. A., Jr (1981) 'How banks can live with low spreads', *Euromoney*, November, 1981, pp. 139–41.

Sachs, J. D. (1981) 'The current account and macroeconomic adjustment in the 1970s', *Brookings Papers on Economic Activity*, Vol. 1, pp. 201–69.

Sealey, C. W., Jr and Lindley, J. T. (1977) 'Inputs, outputs and a theory of production and costs at depository financial institutions', *Journal of Finance*, Vol. 32, pp. 1251–65.

Shapiro, A. C. (1982) 'Risk in international banking', *Journal of Financial and Quantitative Analysis*, Vol. 17, pp. 727-39.

Sjaastad, L. A. (1983) 'International debt quagmire: to whom do we owe it?', *The World Economy*, Vol. 6, pp. 305–24.

Sjaastad, L. (1984) 'Country experience with restructuring incentives: the case of Chile', Paper presented to the Conference on Economic Incentives,

University of Kiel, 18–22 June, 1984.

Solomon, R. (1981) 'The debt of developing countries: another look', *Brookings Papers on Economic Activity*, Vol. 2, pp. 593–606.

Stanyer, P. W. and Whitley, J. A. (1981) 'Financing world payments balances', *Bank of England Quarterly Bulletin*, Vol. 21, June 1981, pp. 187–97.

Swoboda, A. K. (1982) 'International banking: Current issues in perspective', *Journal of Banking and Finance*, Vol. 6, pp. 323–48.

Syvrud, D. E. (1974) *Foundations of Brazilian Economic Growth* (Washington, D.C.: AEI–Hoover Institution Press).

Taggart, R. A. Jr and Greenbaum, S. I. (1978) 'Bank capital and public regulation', *Journal of Money, Credit and Banking*, Vol. 10, May, 1978, pp. 158–69.

Theil, H. (1968–9) 'On the use of information theory concepts in the analysis of financial statements', *Management Science*, Vol. 15 (Theory), pp. 459–80.

Monetary Studies, edited by D. Carson (Homewood, Ill.: Irwin).

Tobin, J. (1965) 'The theory of portfolio selection', in *The Theory of Interest Rates: Proceedings of a Conference Held by the International Economics Association,* edited by F. H. Hahn and F. R. Brechling (New York: Macmillan).

Triffin, R. (1982) 'The European Monetary System and the dollar in the framework of the world monetary system', *Banca Nazionale del Lavoro,* Vol. 35, pp. 245–64.

Wallich, H. C. (1978) 'How much private bank lending is enough?', in *Financing and Risk in Developing Countries,* edited by S. H. Goodman (New York: Praeger).

Weberman B. (1972) 'Techniques of competition', *The Banker,* December 1972, pp. 1, 681.

Whitley, A. (1984) 'Why the World Bank poured money into Brazil', *Financial Times,* 11 September 1984, p. 20.

Wills, H. R. (1982) 'The simple economics of bank regulation', *Economica,* Vol. 49, pp. 249–59.

Index